The New York Times

BEST OF SATURDAY CROSSWORDS

The New York Times

BEST OF SATURDAY CROSSWORDS
75 of Your Favorite Sneaky Saturday Puzzles from
The New York Times

Edited by Will Shortz

ST. MARTIN'S GRIFFIN 🜲 NEW YORK

ACROSS

1 Insignificant row
9 Traffic reporter's aid
15 Big rush, maybe
16 Twin's rival
17 Offerer of stock advice
18 Grown-up who's not quite grown up
19 No big shot?
20 Nasty intentions
22 Threatening word
23 Overseas rebellion cry
25 One may be played by a geisha
26 Wasn't given a choice
27 "You Be ___" (1986 hip-hop hit)
29 Super German?
31 Pressure
33 Launch site
34 Where many airways are cleared, briefly
35 Antithesis of 32-Down
37 Common sound in Amish country
39 Large amount
42 Classics with 389 engines
44 Scrammed
48 Like Fabergé eggs
51 Schoolyard retort
52 Carry ___
53 So great
55 Paving block
56 Golf lesson topic
57 Goes downhill
59 Troubling post-engagement status, briefly
60 Doctor
62 They were labeled "Breakfast," "Dinner" and "Supper"
64 2002 César winner for Best Film
65 Real rubbish
66 Least significant
67 It really gets under your skin

DOWN

1 Determine the value of freedom?
2 Carp
3 Scandinavia's oldest university
4 Sneeze lead-ins
5 Austrian conductor Karl
6 Recess
7 Be quiet, say
8 Savor the flattery
9 It's bad when nobody gets it
10 "The Guilt Trip" actress Graynor
11 Like some cartilage piercings
12 "Possibly"
13 Dream team member
14 Planet threateners
21 Like a top
24 Stain producers
26 Gallant
28 Result of knuckling down?
30 Hollow
32 Antithesis of 35-Across
36 Pageant judging criterion
38 Ed supporters
39 Park Avenue's ___ Building
40 Radical
41 Shaking
43 Sniffing a lot
45 What a slightly shy person may request
46 1967 Emmy winner for playing Socrates
47 "As you like it" phrase
49 What a bunch of footballers might do
50 Game in which the lowest card is 7
54 Marriott rival
57 Preventer of many bites
58 Bit of action
61 Household name?
63 Soreness

by Tom Heilman

2

ACROSS

1 Made a seat-of-the-pants error?
11 "Your mama wears army boots," e.g.
15 Rioting
16 Popular pizza place, informally
17 Washington, D.C., has a famous one
18 Greets enthusiastically, in a way
19 One working in a corner in an office?
20 Eastern Woodlands native
22 Noted eavesdropper, for short
23 Covenants
25 Splendiferous
27 Bar supply
30 ___ Valley
31 Sulky
32 Tandoori-baked fare
34 "Yes" to an invitation
36 One way to stand
37 They may result when you run into people
40 Hognose snake
41 Of two minds
42 ___ work
43 Lender, legally speaking
45 Lo ___
47 50% nonunion?
48 "Gunsmoke" setting
49 Marina sight
51 Classic Northwest brewski
52 Charlie's land
54 Like a tennis match without a break?
58 Like many a gen.
60 Mother of Andromeda
62 "Iliad" locale
63 Settles in, say
64 Job application info, for short
65 Nootropics, more familiarly

DOWN

1 Internet prowlers
2 Hand or foot
3 Cry frequently made with jazz hands
4 Georg von ___
5 Vice president after whom a U.S. city is thought to have been named
6 Ninny
7 Best Picture of 1960, with "The"
8 ___ Palmas
9 Breastplate of Athena
10 "The High One"
11 Where a canine sits?
12 Whole
13 Winter Olympics sight
14 They use blue books
21 TV show headed by a former writer for "S.N.L."

24 "Mom" and "Mama's Family"
26 Poetic expanses
27 Grumpy
28 They use Blue Books
29 "The Wishing-Chair" series creator
33 Manage
35 Whiner, of a sort
38 Kind of compressor
39 Yankee, once
44 Passes
46 "Uh-uh!"
50 #2 pop
53 Title with an apostrophe
55 Appear stunned
56 Apothecary item
57 Din-din
59 Prefix with peptic
61 2 Tone influence

by Michael Ashley

ACROSS

1 Air protection program?
10 Italian alternative
15 Tight squeeze for a couple?
16 Where Union Pacific is headquartered
17 1992 chart-topper that mentions "my little turn on the catwalk"
18 Tar
19 65-Across's title: Abbr.
20 Evian competitor
21 Gun shows?
22 A or O, but not B
24 First name in fashion
26 One going for the big bucks
27 ___ Fund Management (investment company)
29 Strike-monitoring org.
30 Contact on Facebook
31 Time reversal?
33 Tore to shreds
35 Diehard sort
38 Dangerous things to go on
39 Long, slender glass for drinking beer
41 River to the North Sea
42 Lowly one
43 Quarterly magazine published by Boeing
45 Norwegian Romanticist
49 Anti
50 Sch. in Madison, N.J.
52 ___ Gunn, "Breaking Bad" co-star
53 Killing it
56 Make a touchdown
58 Star opening?
59 Turning blue, maybe
60 Prevent a crash, say
62 Triumphant cry
63 "Buy high and sell low," e.g.
64 Baselines?
65 Case worker

DOWN

1 Springblade producer
2 Marmalade fruit
3 Green piece
4 Wall Street inits.
5 ___ Musk, co-founder of Tesla Motors and PayPal
6 Millan who's known as "the Dog Whisperer"
7 Temporarily inactive
8 ___ Place (Edmonton Oilers' arena)
9 Frozen food aisle eponym
10 See 11-Down
11 She loves, in 10-Down
12 "G-Funk Classics" rapper
13 Iroquoian tongue
14 Provincials
21 "Holy smokes!"
23 Long Island Rail Road station
25 Old phone trio
28 Spartan gathering place
30 Bakery/cafe chain
32 Schwab rival
34 Rhames of "Mission: Impossible"
35 Pioneering underground publication of the 1960s
36 Early tragedienne Duse
37 1990s sci-fi series
40 Alternative to die
41 In the direction of
44 Make further advances?
46 Sense
47 Italian P.M. Letta
48 Boot covering
51 Open, in a way
54 Kind of threat
55 Certain spirits
57 Frankie Avalon's "___ Dinah"
60 Org. with a top 10 list
61 Shopper's choice

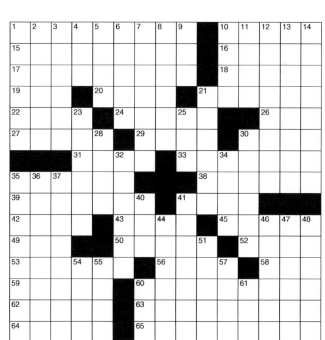

by David Steinberg

4

ACROSS

1 It includes pinning and throwing
8 "Chicago" setting
15 Rapture
16 Skyrocket
17 Prepare to pull the trigger
18 Couple seen at a baby shower
19 Hard knocks
20 It might hold up a holdup
22 Reason for a semiannual shift: Abbr.
23 Skunk and such
24 Star in Virgo
25 Aid in getting a grip
26 Check spec.
27 Abyss
28 Modern Persian
29 "That's clever!"
31 California's ___ Sea (rift lake)
32 Got a 41-Across on
33 Billy who played the Phantom in "The Phantom"
34 Person with small inventions
37 Slam dunk stat
41 Benchmark mark
42 They have seats
43 Crew's director
44 "Que ___-je?" ("What do I know?": Fr.)
45 "The Great Caruso" title role player
46 Perpetual 10-year-old of TV
47 Wile E. Coyote buy
48 Too, to Thérèse
49 Board game with black and white stones
50 Pupil of Pissarro
52 Like many laptop cameras
54 First name among Italian explorers
55 With ramifications
56 Galls
57 Does some farrier's work on

DOWN

1 One feeling 15-Across after Super Bowl III
2 Title name written "on the door of this legended tomb," in poetry
3 Home of Southeast Asia's largest mosque
4 News briefs
5 Colombian kinfolk
6 "___ see"
7 Like the human genome, before the 1990s
8 "St. John Passion" composer
9 Now, to Nicolás
10 Choice for a long shot
11 Sound in the comic "B.C."
12 Groveled
13 Tepid consent
14 Sitcom pal of Barbarino and Horshack
21 Grammy-nominated Ford
24 No-yeast feast
25 Parking meeter?
27 Cuts up
28 Adder's defense
30 They're off-limits: Var.
31 Pole star?
33 Its main island is Unguja
34 Asset in a drag contest
35 Whence a girl who's "like a samba," in song
36 Member of 31-Down's team
37 Geiger of Geiger counter fame
38 "You're not the only one!"
39 Recess for a joint
40 Reaches
42 Leisurely strolls
45 It's often parried
46 Impolite interruption
48 Indigo source
49 Spinal cord surrounders
51 Rescue vessel?
53 Relative of Aztec

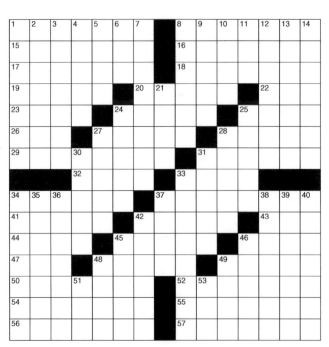

by Frederick J. Healy

ACROSS

1 1960s sitcom character with the catchphrase "I see nothing!"
11 Kvetch
15 Pitchblende, e.g.
16 Disney title character surnamed Pelekai
17 Singles collection?
18 Hostile
19 Malignant acts
20 "Not serious!"
21 Lose one's place?
22 Itches
23 Places gowns are worn, for short
24 Setting for many reprises
26 Elated outpouring
28 Hercules type
29 Result of some fermentation
33 Ingredient in Worcestershire sauce
35 Still in the 17-Across
37 Still
38 Second baseman in both of the Dodgers' 1980s World Series
40 Like South Carolina visa-à-vis North Carolina, politically
41 Storied abductee
42 Sports mascot who's a popular bobblehead figure
44 Ring
46 Comfort's partner
47 "The X Files" project, for short
51 Verb in the world's first telegraph message
52 Watergate units: Abbr.
54 Embroidery loop
55 Brand once pitched by Garfield
56 Where filing work is done

58 Relative of aloha or shalom
59 Home of the WNBA's Silver Stars
60 Transcendental aesthetic developer
61 Accent for plus fours, often

DOWN

1 Like many drafts
2 Lollipop selection
3 Tarte ___ (French apple dessert)
4 Uncooperative moods
5 What César awards honor
6 Stick close to
7 One paid to make calls
8 Considers
9 "Star Trek: T.N.G." role
10 Literary wife in "Midnight in Paris"

11 Nearly set?
12 Judicious state
13 Minor payment
14 Early riser?
23 Locales that may be well-supplied?
25 Digs on a slope
26 Recognition not sought by Benjamin Franklin
27 Rapper with the 2012 album "Life Is Good"
29 Clear one's way, in a way
30 Latin condenser
31 Cookware that's often hinged
32 Cared
34 Overcome by mud
36 Weir
39 Blue label
43 Lose
45 Medieval merchants' guild

47 Grain elevator components
48 Discount, in combination
49 Vodka ___
50 "There, there"
53 "Up to ___" (1952 game show)
54 Fancy spread
57 Show on Sen. Franken's résumé

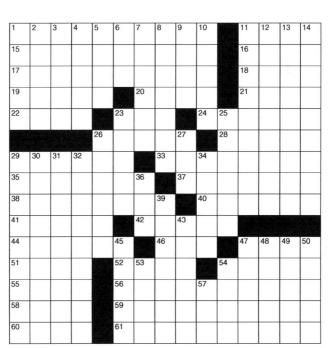

by Byron Walden and Brad Wilber

ACROSS

1 Big name in 25-Across treatment
9 Air piece?
14 Shrugs, maybe
16 Take it as a sign
17 "The Help" co-star, 2011
18 Decorative moldings
19 First of a succession of 13
20 Coot
22 Johnny-jump-up, e.g.
24 Nude medium, often
25 See 1-Across
27 90 degrees from ouest
28 Really
31 Area map
32 ___ d'âme (moods: Fr.)
33 Alternative to 53-Down
34 Secures
37 She's no puritan
40 Farm sounds
41 Station, e.g.
42 Repulsive
43 Get out of practice?
45 Sportscaster Nahan with a star on the Hollywood Walk of Fame
48 Keel extension
49 Unrefined type
50 Key setting
52 Like eggheads
56 Stockholder's group?
57 Universal work
58 Hack, say
60 Nonstop
61 Evidence of having worn thongs
62 Little ones are calves
63 Player of many a tough guy

DOWN

1 Olympian on 2004 and 2012 Wheaties boxes
2 Bach contemporary
3 Onetime pop star who hosted "Pyramid"
4 First name in erotica
5 Fortune subjects: Abbr.
6 Stalin defier
7 Stargazer's focus?
8 Street fair lineup
9 Lodge org.
10 Fryer seen at a cookout?
11 Harvard has an all-male one
12 Creation for many an account
13 Super Mario Bros. runner
15 Backing
21 ___ rating (chess skill-level measure)
23 So-far-undiscovered one
26 Name-dropper's abbr.?
29 Aid in making one's move?
30 So-far-undiscovered ones, briefly
32 Like a type B
34 Geishas often draw them
35 Wimp's lack
36 Wrest the reins
37 Crane arm
38 Ace's stat
39 Open love?
41 To the degree that
43 What mops may be made into
44 Feet with rhythm
45 Dealt with
46 Abercrombie design
47 Brought to ruin
51 Kick back
53 Alternative to 33-Across
54 Ripped
55 Drumroll follower
57 Group with family units
59 Actor Penn of "Van Wilder"

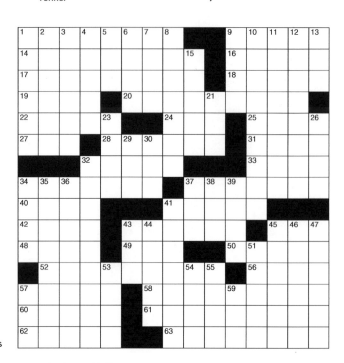

by James Mulhern

ACROSS

1. 2015 Toronto event
11. Office staples
14. Slide
15. Protagonist in David Foster Wallace's "Infinite Jest"
16. "Corpus Christi" playwright
18. Ones united in France?
19. Manufacturer of boxy cars
20. Treasure
21. Loose end?
22. "Return to Never Land" role
23. Darkroom chemical solution
24. Pickle
25. Big gun
26. U.S. city that's almost as large in area as Delaware
35. Part of a French cabinet
36. Jumbo, e.g.
37. Shpilkes
38. Certain shell contents
39. Joan Sebastian's "___ y Más"
40. Pull out all the stops
43. Miracle site
45. Latin primer word
49. Hip to
50. Enterprise Klingon
51. Close call
52. Forrest Tucker's "F Troop" role
55. X-___ large
56. What solidifies things in the end?
57. Member of the E Street Band
58. Bit of forensic evidence

DOWN

1. Golfer Calvin
2. Quattro relatives
3. Quaint complaint
4. Husband of Otrera
5. TV ad unit: Abbr.
6. Not cover one's butt?
7. Formation from glaciation
8. Former first lady
9. List-ending abbrs.
10. When repeated, a breath freshener
11. Jacob's-ladder, for one
12. Make a little lower?
13. More artful
14. Tank gun first produced by the Soviets in W.W. II
17. Ottoman ruler nicknamed "The Lion"
22. 19th-/20th-century U.S. portraitist
23. ___ Brunelleschi, Italian Renaissance architect who developed linear perspective
24. Coupling
25. 1958 41-Down by Samuel Barber
26. Mennen line
27. Scandinavian goddess of fate
28. Suffix with pluto-
29. "Ocean's Eleven" activity
30. Cagney classic of 1935
31. Big name in modeling agencies
32. "South Park" boy
33. The Garden of England
34. Song and dance
40. Flag wavers?
41. 25-Down, for one
42. Common cleanser
43. Neighbor of Gabon
44. Holder of Leia's secret
45. Legend maker
46. Cuban revolutionary José
47. "Little Miss Sunshine" co-star
48. Souvenir buys
50. Keen
51. Flue problem
53. Literary inits.
54. Real-estate listing abbr.

by Martin Ashwood-Smith

8

ACROSS

1 Girl's name in #1 1973 and 1974 song titles
6 With 20-Across, where the first-ever crossword puzzle appeared
13 Reserved parking spaces and others
14 Less light
15 Form of many a birthday cake
16 Jojoba oil is a natural one
17 Lead-in to now
18 Home of MacDill Air Force Base
19 Had ___ (flipped)
20 See 6-Across
24 Legal attachment?
25 Light unit
26 Acclaim for picadors
28 Certain sultan's subjects
30 They're not team players
34 Lab dept.
35 La ___ (California resort and spa)
36 Extended trial
38 Not for the general public
39 Morlocks' enemy
41 Saxony, e.g.
42 Shot
45 Creator of the first crossword
49 Kingdom vanquished by Hammurabi
51 Actor Tom of "The Seven Year Itch"
52 Ranch sobriquet
53 1989 Peace Nobelist
55 Aviary sound
57 To a fault
58 Fruit whose name comes from Arawak
59 Year in which the first crossword appeared, on December 21
60 Firth, e.g.

DOWN

1 Where vaults can be seen
2 Jacket style
3 Noted geographical misnomer
4 "South Park" boy
5 Basic Latin verb
6 Hobbyist, e.g.
7 Jerry Orbach role in "The Fantasticks"
8 Early Chinese dynasty
9 Neighborhood org. since 1844
10 Chilling
11 Mulligans, e.g.
12 Mardi Gras group
14 Big sport overseas?
16 Babe in the woods
18 Sailors' chains
21 City on the Firth of Tay
22 "Star Wars" queen and senator
23 Canine vestigial structure
27 High-hatting
28 Cortés's quest
29 Graffiti, say
31 Like many nutrients
32 1, for one: Abbr.
33 Poor, as an excuse
37 Rock singer?
38 Key never used by itself
40 Formal confession
41 Toni Morrison novel
42 Obscure
43 Like some vin
44 R. J. Reynolds brand
46 Borders
47 Brass
48 Hemingway, notably
50 T. J. ___
54 "Voues êtes ___"
55 Staple of sci-fi filmmaking
56 Ostrogoth enemy

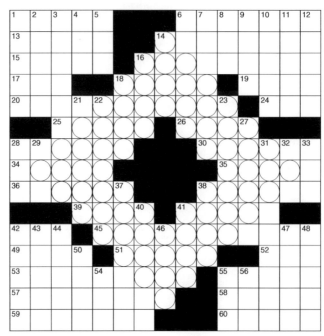

by Todd Gross and David Steinberg

ACROSS

1 Gut-busting side
11 Port. title
15 Alternative to 1-Across
16 Some GPS suggestions, informally
17 Shooting star?
18 College figs.
19 It means little in the Lowlands
20 Trimming gizmo
21 Like floppy disks, e.g.
22 Vino de ___ (Spanish wine designation)
23 Red shade
24 Santa Ana wind source
27 It may be up against the wall
29 Bring out
30 1975 hit song about "tramps like us"
33 Like Athena
34 Sharon's predecessor
35 Fig. for I, O or U, but not A or E
36 It may be said while wearing a toga
38 Manual series
39 Phoenix suburb larger than the Midwest city it's named for
40 Break through
41 Princess of ballet
43 Like red bell peppers
44 Orders
45 Key ring?
47 Scoutmaster, often
50 The moment that
51 It's not drawn due to gravity
53 Co-star in the U.S. premiere of "Waiting for Godot," 1956
54 Pride and joy
55 Abstainers
56 Question from a bully

DOWN

1 Slight pushes
2 One at the U.S. Mint?
3 Jonathan's wife in "Dracula"
4 A.L. East team, on sports tickers
5 Like many pregnant women
6 Where to get a cold comfort?
7 #1 spoken-word hit of 1964
8 "My Son Is a Splendid Driver" novelist, 1971
9 Castle of ___ (Hungarian tourist draw)
10 Old map abbr.
11 Like some pills and lies
12 Dilly
13 Bait
14 Listing on I.R.S. Form 8949
21 Summit success
22 Front runners
23 Engine buildup
24 Sound like a baby
25 Cartoon pooch
26 Hunky-dory
27 Rather informal?
28 Printer part
30 Port on the Adriatic
31 Like Bill Maher, notably
32 Supporter of shades
34 Unembellished
37 Stock to put stock in
38 Verbal alternative to a head slap
40 Go for a car-cramming record, say
41 Anciently
42 Tunisian money
43 ___ presto
45 Devotional period?
46 Insignificant
47 Twain's "celebrated jumping frog"
48 Talent show lineup
49 "___ Bones G'wine Rise Again" (spiritual)
51 Important card source: Abbr.
52 Deterrent to lateness or cancellation

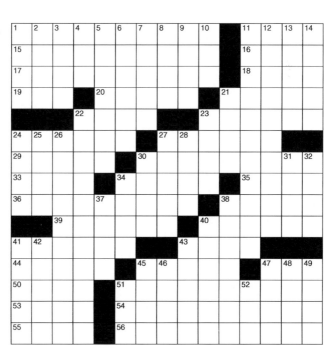

by Frederick J. Healy

ACROSS

1 Like cork trees and flying lizards
6 "Jersey Shore" housemate's music-biz name
14 Jersey Shore vacation option
15 Big Dipper's setting
16 One offering help in passing?
17 Take up enthusiastically
18 See 34-Down
19 Where Lee Harvey Oswald was a lathe operator
20 City where some believe Cain and Abel are buried
21 Warden in drab clothes
23 Take down with a charge
24 Spring event in the Summer Olympics?
25 Setting that makes things right?
27 Less agreeable
30 Be a lush
35 Chicken à la rey?
36 Buzzes, say
38 Tiny amount
39 Was revolting
41 Was a rocker?
43 Tie ___
45 Up
46 Hyperbola parts
50 House meeting place
54 Theoretical
55 Predictor of fame
56 Elasticity
57 School meeting places
59 Photometry unit
60 Be an unhelpful interrogee
61 Lack life
62 Life or death
63 Leaf part

DOWN

1 Go on the fritz
2 Monty Python theme composer
3 Gaps
4 Like cute nerds, in slang
5 "___ did you nothing hear?": Hamlet
6 Stress, to Strauss
7 First-class regulars
8 Keeping buff?
9 Jock: Abbr.
10 Raider in the battle of the St. Lawrence
11 "___ Paw" (Oscar-winning Disney short)
12 "Eyewitness" director Peter
13 Hurdy-gurdy sound
15 Flashed
19 Tuareg rebellion locale of 2012
22 Erase
26 Three-ring setting
27 Some rescue work
28 Neighbor of Rabbit
29 Bunk
31 Foreshadow
32 One not getting benefits, say
33 Make baloney?
34 With 18-Across, software developer's concern
37 Constituent of molding sand
40 Touching scene at an airport?
42 Animation
44 European president who attended Harvard
46 Bank
47 Path
48 One of 64 in a genetic table
49 Piece of work
51 Napoleon, notably
52 Where things may be heating up
53 Molto adagio
58 Bit of sportswear
59 Head

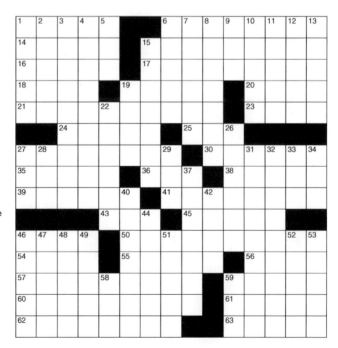

by Kyle Dolan

ACROSS

1 It has a close "Kentucky" cousin
16 Tax deferral options
17 Water gun fight?
18 Tumblers
19 Nonprofessional
20 "Thus weary of the world, away she ___": Shak.
21 Burnable medium, briefly
23 Slender runner
25 One may remove grease with elbow grease
30 SC Johnson brand
32 Does a Ludacris impersonation
34 Grid great Greasy
35 Not the least bit
37 "That's expensive!"
39 Sum symbol
40 Rice alternative
42 Stop on Amtrak's California Zephyr
43 Dead player?
45 Key contraction
46 ___ ed
47 Larry of the original "West Side Story"
49 Went nowhere
51 They're usually pixelated on TV
59 Kelp is a natural source of it
60 One who orders trunks to be moved?
61 Member of a drill team?

8 Sawmill supplier
9 Fish in a dragon roll
10 They have bills and appear on bills
11 Renowned boxing gym in Brooklyn
12 Outer limits
13 Diomedes speared him
14 Having good balance
15 They were retired in '03
21 Like new notes
22 Freshwater aquarium favorite
23 Many a dama: Abbr.
24 Deck
26 Brand
27 Renaissance composer of "Missa Papae Marcelli"
28 How troglodytes live
29 Clean out

31 DiMaggio and others
33 Fitting decision
36 Wisconsin county or its seat
38 A.L. East team, on scoreboards
41 Really cheap shots?
44 Monthly
48 Spanish royal
49 Attic promenades
50 Book review?
51 Weigh-in section?
52 Woody trunk
53 Korean War weapon
54 Abbr. by Hook or by Cook
55 Drs. often take over for them
56 iPhone talker
57 Fall scene
58 Fundació Joan Miró designer

DOWN

1 U.P.S. deliveries: Abbr.
2 Poor as ___ (destitute)
3 Belly dancers' bands?
4 Native of Caprica on "Battlestar Galactica"
5 Corker
6 Done to ___
7 Alternatives to racks

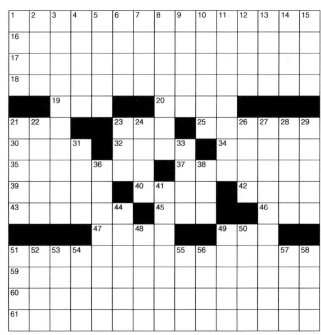

by Martin Ashwood-Smith

ACROSS

1 Fast-paced alternative to Scrabble
12 Lance cpl.'s org.
15 It has a Page Navigation menu option
16 100 sawbucks
17 Cop car, to a CBer
18 Inhibiter of free speech
19 Exchange some words?
20 Follower of Bush or Clinton
21 Many an Israeli
23 Part of some bargain store names
24 Do-or-die situation
27 ___-to-be
28 Green on a screen
30 Texas' ___ Duro Canyon
31 High style of the 1700s
32 Oppenheimer's agcy.
34 Vocal trio
36 1983 song with the lyric "Let's leave Chicago to the Eskimos"
40 Women, poetically, with "the"
41 Nonverbal equivalent of "You have got to be kidding me!"
43 Cannes neighbors?
44 Financier Kreuger called the Match King
45 Start another tour
47 "Man!"
50 Alternative to nuts?
51 Like 36 of this puzzle's answers
53 Grease monkey's pocket item
55 Formal identification
57 Mix for a mixer
58 Draw to an end
59 Spanish gentleman
60 Professional organizers?
64 Fidelity offering, briefly
65 Feature of 007's car
66 Cornerback Law and others
67 Beyoncé alter ego

DOWN

1 Katharine Lee ___, "America the Beautiful" lyricist
2 Court wear, maybe
3 "I swear, man!"
4 Have an edge against
5 Its website has lesson plans, briefly
6 Vintage fabric
7 Get set
8 Sharp knock
9 Org. whose members look down in the mouth?
10 Its flag has an eagle in the center: Abbr.
11 Some foreign misters
12 Wear that was one of "Oprah's Favorite Things" four times
13 Circumnavigator's way
14 "Transformers" actress, 2007
22 Impugn
24 Call from a tree
25 Tenor ___
26 Trio in Greek myth
29 Round houses?
33 Bow no longer shot
35 Hits with wit
36 2007 book subtitled "Confessions of the Killer"
37 John's place
38 Simple winds
39 "The Twilight Saga" vampire
42 "A Severed Head" novelist, 1961
46 Itinerary start
48 Thing taken to a slip
49 Ulcer treater
52 Mad bit
54 Beau chaser?
56 Endings of rock names
58 One way to crack
61 1977 Steely Dan title track
62 One side in some chalk talks
63 One might show muscles, in brief

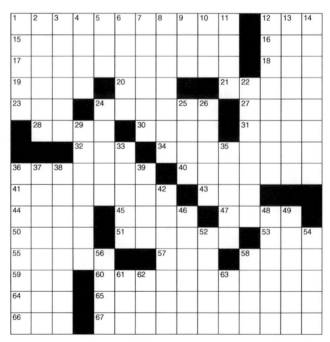

by David Steinberg

ACROSS

1 Body that doesn't remain at rest?
7 Having way too much on one's plate
14 It's not normal
16 Dismissive confession follower
17 Start liking a lot
18 Rare electee
19 ___ B
20 Ingredient in an Americano
22 Like Fabergé eggs
23 Repeated battle cry
25 Megadyne fractions
27 Chef DiSpirito
29 Dog it
30 Texts, e.g.: Abbr.
34 "The Valley of Amazement" novelist, 2013
36 Org. for female shooters
38 Inuit knife
39 Writer of the ethnography "Germania"
41 Get out of the blasted state?
43 What isn't the small print?: Abbr.
44 Suffocating blanket
46 Get off the drive, say
47 Food factory stock
49 Ninny
51 Utter
52 20th-century treaty topic
55 Priceline possibilities
56 Release
59 2012 Pro Bowl player Chris
61 Once-common "commonly"
62 Game that can't be played
64 She wrote "The Proper Care and Feeding of Husbands"

66 "Spread the happy" sloganeer
67 Queen's weapon
68 Producing zip
69 Strips at a pageant

DOWN

1 Given a 20 for food, say
2 Drink that often makes a person sick
3 Road hog
4 Record label abbr.
5 Johns of Britain
6 John of Britain
7 Recife-to-Rio dir.
8 Bible
9 Like Huns
10 Refusal to speak
11 Flatten, as a rivet
12 Throw out
13 Keep from

15 Demonstrate a wide range on a range?
21 Gone private?
24 Early CliffsNotes subheading
26 Restin' piece?
28 Energy bar ingredients
31 "You guessed it . . ."
32 Like some diets that avoid pasta
33 People people
35 Ninny
37 Lincoln and others
40 Diesel discharge
42 Primary and secondary, briefly
45 Bunches
48 Habitual high achiever?
50 Label stable
53 C.D.C. concern
54 "Phooey!"

56 Some heavy planters
57 Like some flags: Abbr.
58 Not full-bodied
60 "Modern Gallantry" pen name
63 Swimming gold medalist Park ___-hwan
65 Key component: Abbr.

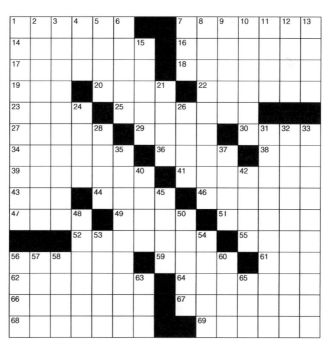

by James Mulhern

14

ACROSS

1 Her 1994 memoir has the chapter "Desert Storm"
12 Plant visitor
15 What watts and volt-amperes have
16 Elementary education, briefly
17 High interest?
18 Choice for a portrait
19 U.K. honours
20 What you may open the door for
21 Aftermath
22 Fun time
23 Toddler coddler
24 Display options, briefly
25 Serpent with a Zulu name
26 Zany
28 On track to win
31 Use pumice on, perhaps
33 He wrote of a "vorpal blade"
35 Gets to a seat, say
36 Member of the German Expressionist group Die Brücke
38 Sky boxes?
39 Exhibit explainer
40 Strawberry, for one
42 Tom Clancy's "Every __ Tiger"
43 Polaris or Procyon
44 Persian language unit?
47 "The Wizard of Oz" farmhand
48 Psychoanalyst Melanie
49 Hometown of the mathematician Fibonacci
50 Much like
51 Words accompanying a low bow
53 X or Y lead-in

54 Uno's alternative
55 Suzanne, e.g.: Abbr.
56 Light insufficiently

DOWN

1 Muddle
2 Great Rift Valley port
3 Dodges
4 Some 27-Down
5 Prefix with culture
6 Like some inspections
7 Danger dinger
8 Old Sony format
9 Come together
10 Cock-a-leekie eater
11 Incubator
12 Sent out in waves?
13 Composer of several "Gnossiennes"
14 Man's name that sounds noble
21 Cooperation exclamation

23 "___ With the Long Neck" (Parmigianino painting)
24 Pro athlete in purple and gold
25 Cary's "Blonde Venus" co-star
26 Dispenser of Duff Beer
27 Desk set
28 Made no mistakes on
29 No breakfast for a vegan
30 TV antiheroine for 41 years
32 One whose shifts shift
34 Development site
37 Warrant
41 Handle
43 Subject to change
44 Screw up
45 Business fraudster Billie Sol ___

46 General who won 1794's Battle of Fallen Timbers
47 Navigates a switchback, in part
48 Severinsbrücke's city
49 One may be fingered
51 "Revolution" or "Hound Dog" starter
52 Port named after a U.S. president, informally

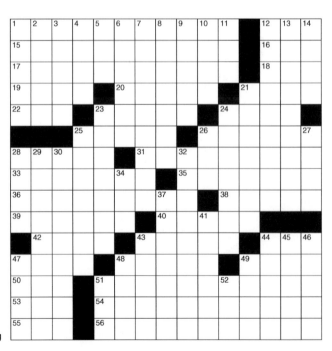

by Will Nediger

ACROSS

1 Things millions of people have received in history?: Abbr.
4 Snap
15 Dieter's beef?
16 Foreigner hit in the musical film "Rock of Ages"
17 ___ poco (soon: It.)
18 Western way
19 Guy
21 Youngest player to qualify for an L.P.G.A. Tour event
22 Ain't fixed?
23 Ticket number?
24 Lock combinations?
25 Jewish community org.
26 Running back's target
27 Five minutes in a campaign itinerary, maybe
29 Physics class subj.
30 Chestnut, say
31 2013 Spike Jonze love story
34 Piece in a fianchetto opening
36 Squalid
38 Yo-yo
39 Play with someone else's toy?
43 "Check it out!," in Chihuahua
44 Induces a shudder in
45 Hominy makers extract it
46 One attached to a handle
48 Decks
49 Something a baton carrier might pick up
50 ___ passu (on equal footing)
51 Head, for short
52 This point forward
53 Sri Lankan export
56 Day of the week of the great stock market crash, Oct. 29, 1929

57 It once had many satellites in its orbit
58 Prefix with -gram
59 Prized cuts
60 Nutritional inits.

DOWN

1 Biblical figure famously painted nude by Rembrandt
2 Certain temple locale
3 Not likely to blush
4 Steep-sided inlet
5 It may be on the line
6 Nickname on old political buttons
7 Watchmaker's cleaning tool
8 Threesome needed in Wagner's "Ring" cycle
9 Bar ___
10 Call routing abbr.

11 Peewee
12 Useful item if you 39-Across
13 "Three Sisters" sister
14 Fool
20 Tree with burs
24 Shipping choice
25 Protest vehemently
27 Low-priced American vodka known affectionately (and ironically) as "Russia's finest"
28 Brewers' hot spots
31 Music genre of Poison and Guns N' Roses
32 Poet arrested for treason in 1945
33 Golden Globes nominee who was a Golden Gloves boxer
35 River through Silesia

37 Reddish remnant
40 Quit working
41 Austrian neighbor
42 "___ alive!"
44 Curb
46 Health store snack ingredient
47 "Inside the Actors Studio" channel
49 Nancy Drew never left hers behind
50 Honeycomb maker
51 "I'm game"
52 Left or right, say
54 "No kiddin'!"
55 "The Power to Surprise" sloganeer

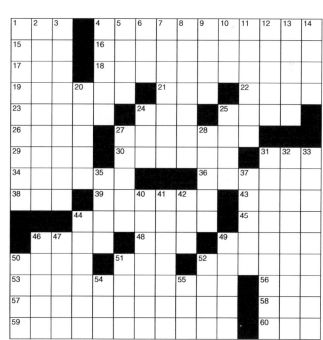

by Doug Peterson and Brad Wilber

16

ACROSS

1 Position papers?
10 Joneses
15 Vanity case?
16 When Epifanía is celebrated
17 Picayune
18 Not barred
19 Low prime, in Paris
20 Newfoundland, in Naples and Nogales
22 Grp. that suspended Honduras from 2009 to '11
24 Messages using Stickies, say
25 Certain guy "ISO" someone
28 Emmy-nominated show every year from 2006 to '09
32 Suffix with 18-Across
33 Just-once link
35 Beta testers, e.g.
36 Steely Dan's title liar
37 One blowing up a lottery machine?
38 Prozac alternative
39 Winnebago relative
40 Odds and ends
41 Clan female
42 Mexican president Enrique __ Nieto
43 Clear
44 Crane settings
46 Van follower, often
47 Japanese guitar brand
49 Toy type, for short
51 Flippers, e.g.
55 Members of a joint task force?
59 "It's __ wind . . ."
60 Dole
62 Green with five Grammys
63 Writer of the graphic novel "Watchmen"
64 Home to the Villa Hügel
65 Outdoor contemplation location

DOWN

1 Didn't spoil
2 Sun or stress
3 MSG ingredient?
4 Certain DNA test
5 Follows a physical request?
6 __ vez más (over again: Sp.)
7 Photoshop addition
8 Mention on Yelp, say
9 Aspire PC maker
10 Tycoon Stanford
11 Bridge opening option, briefly
12 Managed to get through
13 Where to read a plot summary?
14 Totally out
21 Overnight activity
23 Iconic "Seinfeld" role

25 Eighth-century Apostle of Germany
26 Old collar stiffeners
27 Engagement parties?
29 Company that added four letters to its name in 1997
30 Sides in a classic battle
31 Longtime Cincinnati Pops conductor Kunzel
34 Pavement caution
36 One of a silent force?
44 Longtime name in banking
45 Its seat is Santa Rosa
48 Lawyer on "Ally McBeal"
50 No modest abode
52 2009 Grammy winner for "Make It Mine"
53 Farm block

54 "Mr. Mom" director Dragoti
56 Cross
57 Purpose of many a shot
58 Old carbine
61 End to end?

by Julian Lim

ACROSS

1 Ones who think things are good as gold?
11 Like metals used by 1-Across
15 Feared sight on the Spanish Main
16 Obama's favorite character on "The Wire"
17 Like some parents
18 Big long-distance carrier?
19 Coastal fish consumers
20 Much may follow it
21 Composer of the opera "Rusalka"
23 Deal with
25 People might pass for them, for short
27 High line in the Middle East
28 Small cell
30 Brand of body washes
32 Grp. with the Office of Iraq Analysis
33 Art that uses curse words?
37 Volt-ampere
38 Takes the plunge
39 Peak transmission setting of old?
41 Declines, with "out"
42 Fall apart
44 Score abbr.
45 First name of Woodstock's last performer
46 Split second?
47 Golden, in Granada
49 Hit with skits, for short
51 Get off the drive, say
55 No-gooder
57 2012 baseball All-Star Kinsler
59 Some plans for the future, briefly
60 Rackets
61 High spirits?
64 Land capturer, in literature
65 "Bummer"
66 Tied
67 Whip wielder

DOWN

1 Vaulted areas
2 Tall order at a British pub
3 Big picker-upper?
4 Frequent Monet subjects
5 Projection in the air, for short
6 Kind of bust
7 "___ a man in Reno" ("Folsom Prison Blues" lyric)
8 Well-trained boxer, maybe
9 Punk rocker Armstrong with a 2012 Grammy
10 Reached 100, say
11 Near to one's heart
12 First drink ever ordered by James Bond
13 Do-gooder
14 Composer called a "gymnopédiste"
22 Woe, in Yiddish
24 Symbols of might
26 Scuzz
29 Facebook connections in Florence?
31 Start sputtering, say
33 Aid in fast networking
34 One getting messages by word of mouth?
35 Site of the 1992 Republican National Convention
36 Very small (and very important) matter
37 Like some missed field goals
40 Weapon in "The Mikado"
43 Telejournalist's item
45 Part of many a training regimen
48 Plant in subsequent seasons
50 "Swing Shift" Oscar nominee
52 In the back
53 Game stew
54 Locale of London Stansted Airport
56 "Good ___ A'mighty!"
58 Side in an Indian restaurant
62 Certain sorority chapter
63 Tapping grp.

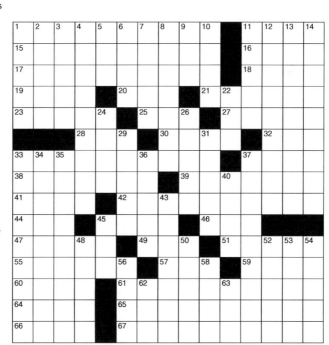

by Evan Birnholz

18

ACROSS

1 1987 #1 hit with the line "Yo no soy marinero, soy capitán"
8 Throwback
15 Samsung Galaxy Note rival
16 Go-ahead for un hombre
17 Forward to some followers
18 Curt chat closing
19 Where Melville's Billy Budd went
20 Hubble sighting
22 Jesse Jackson, for one: Abbr.
24 Like some double-deckers
28 One's own worst critic?
32 Put off
34 Dayton-to-Toledo dir.
35 Subjected to venomous attacks?
38 Four roods
40 Pawnbroker, in slang
41 Travel safety grp.
42 Modern device seen on a bridge
45 L.A. law figure
46 Take a little hair off, maybe
47 To date
49 Den delivery
52 Beats by ___ (brand of audio equipment)
53 One picking up speed, say?
55 They're game
59 Sack dress?
63 Dish often served with a tamarind sauce
65 Disc protector
66 Carrier with a pink logo
67 Like some stockings
68 If it's repeated, it's nothing new

DOWN

1 Turkey tip?
2 Burlesques
3 Moderate
4 Norton AntiVirus target
5 Tina Turner's real middle name
6 Welcome message to international travelers
7 Danza, e.g.
8 Invite to one's penthouse
9 Proof of purchase
10 Ghanaian region known for gold and cocoa
11 Needle or nettle
12 Having five sharps
13 ___ milk
14 III, in Rome
21 Novel groups?
23 They make quick admissions decisions, for short
25 Ink
26 Come by
27 Openly admitted, as in court
28 They sometimes lead to runs
29 Straighten out
30 Italian brewer since 1846
31 Blood members, e.g.
33 Fund
36 Spirit
37 Emmy category, informally
39 Food brand originally called Froffles
43 Photog
44 Cry with a salute
48 Ignored
50 Fade out
51 Like loose stones
54 Decides
56 ___ Drive, thoroughfare by the Lincoln Memorial in Washington
57 Modern posting locale
58 Produced stories
59 .doc alternative
60 Bird: Prefix
61 The Clintons' degs.
62 Cousin of "verdammt"
64 Suffix with official or fan

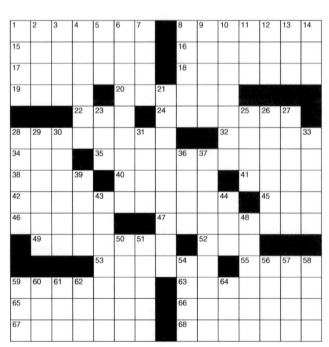

by Ian Livengood and J.A.S.A. Crossword Class

ACROSS

1 Cooler idea?
10 Home to the Great Mosque
15 It included a moonwalk
16 Spirit of St. Petersburg?
17 One stocking bars
18 West African capital
19 Old sitcom sot
20 Pimienta's partner
21 Many instant message recipients
22 "Sketches" pseudonym
23 Bad-tempered
25 Compress, as a file
26 Turn the air blue
28 Where many games can be viewed
29 Prefix with data
30 Motor problems
32 Fat-derived
34 Havana highball
37 Recite mechanically
38 Swank
40 Word before red
41 Beech house?
42 Quarter of zwölf
44 Tables in western scenes
48 Word after red
49 Like time, inexorably
51 "___ I forsook the crowded solitude": Wordsworth
52 Walters portrayer on "S.N.L."
54 Dance piece?
55 Thé addition
56 Produce sentimental notes?
57 Big-name Web crawler
59 "The Asphalt Jungle" revolves around one
60 Like Francisco Goya
61 "Breaking Away" director
62 She "made a fool of everyone," in song

DOWN

1 A. J. ___, author of the best seller "The Know-It-All: One Man's Humble Quest to Become the Smartest Person in the World"
2 Director of "The 40-Year-Old Virgin" and "This Is 40"
3 Turn positive, say
4 Some Yale degs.
5 Nellie who wrote "Ten Days in a Mad-House"
6 Martini accompanier?
7 Uses a drunkometer, e.g.
8 Provençal spreads
9 100-at currency unit
10 It was run during the 1980s–'90s
11 Abbr. for the listless?
12 Tab alternative
13 Big name in allergy relief
14 It's flown in
21 ___ Anne's (pretzel maker)
23 Ultra ___
24 Quick missions?
27 Slightly biased?
29 Like some finishes
31 Hole in one on a par 5 hole
33 "No ___ is worse than bad advice": Sophocles
34 Bahrain, Bhutan or Brunei
35 Clearing
36 Popular line of footwear?
39 Endurance race, briefly
40 Cardiff Giant, e.g.
43 Cry for another piece
45 Starfish setting
46 Some opera passages
47 Parlor piece
49 Word on a restroom door
50 Loose
53 Thing twitched on "Bewitched"
55 River known for the goldfields in its basin
57 Sign on an interstate
58 "___ Tarantos" (1963 film)

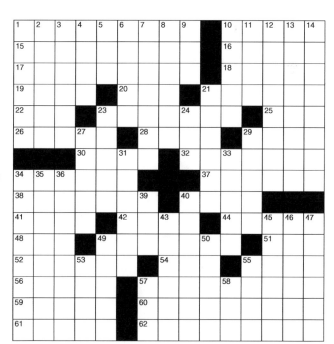

by David Steinberg

ACROSS

1 Like some methods of detection
10 Winter athletes' pull-ups?
15 Without requiring scrutiny
16 Last name in the skin care industry
17 Indication that one wants to get smacked
18 Producer of "whirlybirds"
19 How the descriptions of most things usually end?
20 Cast
21 Like many taxis
22 Bathhouse square
23 N.B.A. team starting in 1988
24 A line, e.g.
27 A lines, e.g.
28 "Essays in Love" writer ___ de Botton
29 People everywhere
32 Since 2010 it's had a shield on its back
33 Buckles
34 Jack for Jacques?
35 Two or three in a row, say
37 Texas state tree
38 Prevent from having anything?
39 What cookies are often baked in
40 Stung
42 Swiss bank depositor?
43 Spare change collector
44 Spare change collectors
45 Vineyard, in Vichy
48 Song of exultation
49 Sexy
51 Failed in a big way
52 Seaweed used in home brewing
53 Some men's sizes
54 One controlling drones

DOWN

1 Relative of a haddock
2 Uplifting company?
3 Bad way to finish
4 Classic two-seaters
5 Blissful
6 Without incident, say
7 Lacking a point
8 A teller might update it: Abbr.
9 Connection between Obama and Robinson?
10 Member of the marmoset family
11 Cold discomfort, of sorts
12 Poppycock
13 Found new tenants for
14 Polar bearers?
21 They're often accompanied by "Hava Nagila"
22 Penalty for some overly prolific posters
23 Rope and dope sources
24 Body bags?
25 Title 54-Across of film
26 Skin behind a slip, perhaps
27 Less likely to have waffles
29 Like supervillains
30 Grape, Cherry or Strawberry lead-in
31 A lot of the time?
33 Need for life
36 Staples of Marvel Comics
37 Cayenne producer
39 Velvety pink
40 Annual winter honoree, briefly
41 Modern two-seater
42 Murphy of "To Hell and Back"
44 "Zzz" inducer
45 Something to buy into
46 Device
47 Miracle on Ice loser of '80
49 Crab house accessory
50 "___ Wed" (2007 Erica Durance movie)

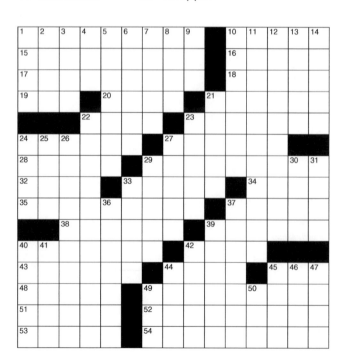

by Ed Sessa

ACROSS

1 Passed in a blur, say
7 Develops gradually
15 Smoking
16 Change-making
17 Where to look for self-growth
18 Obsolescent storage device
19 Historic first name in W.W. II
20 Locale of three presidential libraries
21 Fried
22 One often behind bars
24 Ditch
25 Doesn't carry on
26 Oxygen's lack
27 Rescuer of Princess Peach
28 Near: Fr.
29 Churchyard gravedigger
30 Signs of things to come
34 Truckloads
35 Hard to grasp
36 Remains after the aging process
37 Opposite of 28-Down
38 Santa's reindeer, e.g.
39 Some sharp words
43 Lou's "La Bamba" co-star
44 Concord concoction
46 Many a "Meet the Press" guest, informally
47 Swindler's moola
48 Hiked
49 She had a single-season stint on "The View"
51 Many a worker at Union Pacific headquarters
52 Like Enterprise vehicles
53 Fired up?
54 Best, as friends
55 One of Leakey's "Trimates"

DOWN

1 Decorated band along a wall
2 "Reality leaves a lot to the imagination" speaker
3 He directed Bela Lugosi in "Bride of the Monster"
4 High rollers, in casino lingo
5 Cheap, shoddy merchandise
6 Financial statement abbr.
7 Outdoor wedding settings
8 Alchemist's offering
9 Green party V.I.P.?
10 Three Stooges creator Healy and others
11 Concourse abbr.
12 Personalize for
13 Picture
14 Troopers' toppers
20 Almanac info
23 Large pack
24 Get set to take off
27 What an 18-Across's capacity is measured in, briefly
28 Opposite of 37-Across
29 Message sometimes written below "F"
30 Regular embarkation location
31 Series starter
32 Left
33 "___ se habla español"
34 Did an entrechat
36 Flier
38 Voice lesson subjects
39 Protection for flowers in bud
40 Socially dominant sorts
41 Dirty rat
42 Biggest city on the smallest continent
44 Diving bird
45 Mammoth
47 Cookout irritant
50 ___ root (math quantity)
51 Bungler

by Greg Johnson

ACROSS

1 It's made from an ear and put in the mouth
12 Highlander's accessory
15 1967 hit by the Hollies
16 One may have a full body
17 Copied the page?
18 They often land next to queens: Abbr.
19 Prefix with flop
20 They often land next to queens
22 Cross quality
23 Move a whole lot
25 Backward
26 Fame
29 Spice stores?
31 Enigmatic
34 Nanny, in Nanjing
35 Question after a surprising claim
36 Party bowlful
37 Supply one's moving address?
38 Network point
39 Now whole
41 Orphaned lion of literature
42 Knit at a social function?
43 Brownie alternative
45 "Veep" airer
46 Pinch-hitter
49 Smallest member of the Council of Europe
52 See 7-Down
53 Withdraw
54 It's between Buda and Pest
57 After
58 Forum setting
59 180
60 Target of a spy

DOWN

1 Herder from Wales
2 Live warning?
3 Voice lesson topic
4 Bulldogs play in it: Abbr.
5 86
6 Rush target
7 With 52-Across, something in a gray area
8 Himalayan production
9 Golfer Aoki
10 Ayn Rand, e.g.
11 Higher-up?
12 Target
13 Every second
14 Jam
21 Product of some decay
23 O's is one more than N's
24 Comb composition
26 Like some pitches
27 Orders
28 Locals call it the "Big O"
30 Where spades may be laid down
31 End of a song often sung by inebriated people
32 Shark's place
33 Polar Bear Provincial Park borders it
37 Minestrone ingredient
39 Repetitive
40 Bunch
44 Self-congratulatory cries
46 Not just wolf down
47 "I'd love to help"
48 Part of Che Guevara's attire
49 Junior in 12 Pro Bowls
50 Highlander of old
51 Period sans soleil
52 Magazine fig.
55 Half of nine?
56 U.S.P.S. assignment

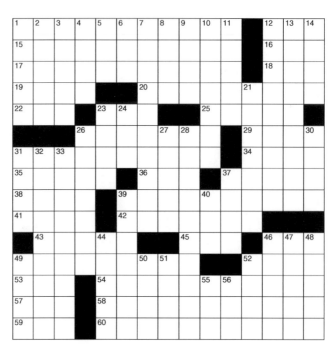

by Barry C. Silk

ACROSS

1. "That's crazy, dude!"
5. Drive to drink, e.g.
15. It's best to stay out of its way
16. Debut Peter Tosh album, and a rallying cry for pot smokers
17. Scheme for the start of a sonnet
18. Opinion leader?
19. Pioneer of New Journalism
21. "r u there?," e.g.
22. Unpolished pro?
23. Stationary
24. Cro-Magnon orphan of literature
25. Head turner
26. Rihanna or Sharon Stone
28. Big name in late-night TV
29. See 25-Down
30. Dandy
31. Ripped
32. U.S. Open champion whose last name is a toy
34. Artist and chess player who said "While all artists are not chess players, all chess players are artists"
38. The end?
39. It takes time to cure
40. McDonald's denial
41. The end
44. It involves hand-to-hand coordination
46. Souls
47. Wish-Bone alternative
48. Lodging portmanteau
49. 1967 Calder Trophy winner at age 18
50. ___ Epstein, baseball V.I.P. known as "Boy Wonder"
51. Last name in "Star Wars"
52. Singer with the 1996 triple-platinum album "Tidal"
55. Panache
56. Where Jason Kidd played college hoops
57. Rap's ___ Yang Twins
58. 1996 Rhett Akins country hit
59. Store whose shoe department has its own ZIP code (10022-SHOE)

DOWN

1. "Yes?"
2. Certain chili
3. Third degree for a third degree?
4. One may prefer them to blondes
5. Bit of ballet instruction
6. Like Tickle Me Elmo
7. "My treat"
8. Parent company?
9. Internet traffic statistics company
10. Pleasant cadence
11. Strong arm
12. Joint
13. Buckle
14. Forever in the past?
20. Up-to-date
24. Like some seamen
25. With 29-Across, nest egg choice
27. Cockerdoodle, e.g.
28. "Oh goody!"
31. Clipped
33. Young foxes
34. Certain gumdrops
35. It was home to two Wonders of the Ancient World
36. Earn a load of money, in modern lingo
37. Some kitchen detritus
39. Impressive range
41. Tool
42. Fortify
43. Oxygen user
44. Imitated chicks
45. Carnival items served with chili
47. Yellow-brown shade
50. Fictional home five miles from Jonesboro
51. A through G
53. Duck Hunt platform, briefly
54. Historical figure aka Marse Robert

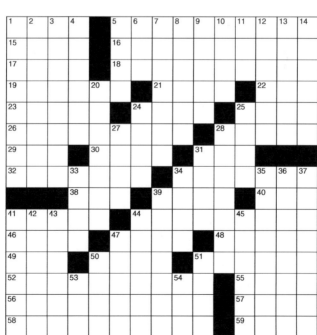

by Ashton Anderson and James Mulhern

24

ACROSS

1 Popularity boost due to a certain TV endorsement
12 Rebel in a beret
15 "A thousand pardons"
16 Athlete in a shell
17 Diet, e.g.
18 "Collages" novelist, 1964
19 Arab spring?
20 Mexicans roll them
21 Composers of some rhapsodies
23 Business of 41-Down: Abbr.
24 Wear for Hu Jintao
25 Mythical abode of heroes slain in battle
29 "Each of us bears his own Hell" writer
30 Part of a drag outfit
31 Relatives of black holes
34 Cousin of an agave
35 Dispatch
36 To you, in Toulouse
37 Place for rank-and-filers in the House of Commons
39 Ozone menace
40 Pungent panini ingredient
41 Gets started
42 They often provide illumination in galleries
44 Arm with many vessels, maybe
45 Like angels
46 Palooka
47 Throws for a loop
51 Shakespeare sonnet that begins "So am I as the rich, whose blessed key"
52 Parts of some alarms
55 Fleece
56 White whale's whereabouts

57 Bath setting: Abbr.
58 People sampling mushrooms, say

DOWN

1 Druid, e.g.
2 Spanning
3 Theme of several theme parks
4 Piltdown man, say
5 Dot-dot-dot
6 Casualty of the Battle of Roncesvalles
7 Old dynasts
8 Some spam senders
9 The Negro R. runs through it
10 "Fantasy Island" host
11 Stray mongrels
12 Chancellery settings
13 Where Nord, Nord-Est and Nord-Ouest are departments

14 Arp contemporary
22 "Interesting . . . but museum-worthy?"
23 Org. whose logo has an eagle and scales
24 Opposite of gloom
25 King of Kings
26 1987 Lionel Richie hit
27 21st-century pastime for treasure hunters
28 Leonov who was the first man to walk in space
29 Balboa's first name
31 Alternative to shoots?
32 A cube has one
33 ___-Soviet
35 Like many a purple-tinged moorland
38 "Fur Traders Descending the Missouri" painter, 1845

39 Creator of "30 Rock"
41 Its parent is Liberty Mutual
42 Opposite of agitato
43 Pizza topping
44 Pizza topping
46 Bart and Lisa's bus driver
47 Sacs studied by 58-Across
48 Parts of a sob story
49 Latin 101 word
50 Phishing loot: Abbr.
53 Orange's org.
54 Periodic dairy aisle offering

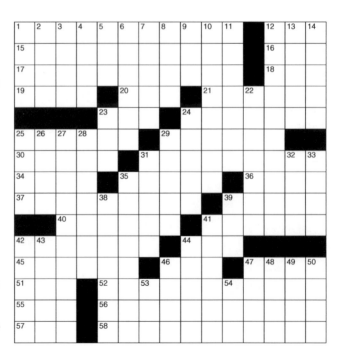

by Mel Rosen

ACROSS

1 Simpler
16 Sequential
17 Harry Potter series part
18 Can't take
19 One of a familiar septet
20 Rocks on the Rhein?
21 Gabriel García Márquez's "Cien ___ de Soledad"
22 Weapon in old hand-to-hand combat
23 Figures in "Teutonic Mythology"
25 "Vous êtes ___"
26 Alaska's ___ Fjords National Park
27 Candy pioneer H. B. ___
28 Abbr. in many a military title
29 Small skillet
31 Abbr. before a date
32 Big Chicago-based franchiser
33 1958–61 political alliance: Abbr.
35 March on Washington grp.
38 Dirgelike
42 20-Across in English
45 Blush
47 Not a good person to entrust with secrets, informally
48 And moreover
49 Answer (for)
50 Goya figure
51 Part of a plowing harness
52 Problem for Poirot
53 Quickly imagine?
55 Swiss city that borders France and Germany
56 Spotless
59 Boos, e.g.
60 "Different strokes for different folks"

DOWN

1 Either of two Holy Roman emperors
2 Better
3 "Get cracking!"
4 White-bearded types
5 Some budget planners, for short
6 Gambling inits.
7 Putting one's cards on the table, in a way
8 Package for sale, say
9 Principal port of Syria
10 "___ out?"
11 Strongbox
12 Raiding grp.
13 Robin Hood and his Merry Men
14 Otherworldly in the extreme
15 Decent
22 "Portraits at the Stock Exchange" artist
24 Look that's not liked
26 ___ party
30 ___ York
32 Seattle's Space Needle or St. Louis's Gateway Arch
34 Something that often follows you
35 Greta of "The Red Violin"
36 Hardly any
37 Immediate, as relatives
39 Seeps
40 Actress in "Ferris Bueller's Day Off"
41 Decorate fancily
42 Bothered
43 Broadway hit with the song "I Wonder What the King Is Doing Tonight"
44 Telescope part
46 Mezzo-soprano Regina
51 Must
54 Blanched
55 Inexpensive writing implements
57 ___ price
58 Bad computer?

by Stu Ockman

ACROSS

1 "Friday the 13th" setting
5 Cry accompanying a slap
15 Green leader?
16 Office addresses?
17 Tragically heartbroken figure of myth
18 Some cocktail garnishes
19 Noted nominee of 2005
21 Stumped
22 Bit of audio equipment?
23 Controversial thing to play
25 Stats. for new arrivals
27 Base's opposite
29 "That's true—however . . ."
33 Locale for the Zoot Suit Riots of '43
36 Fashion clothes
38 Team unifier
39 They created the Get Rid of Slimy GirlS club
42 Brand with a "Wonderfilled" ad campaign
43 Nail
44 Beginning of some tributes
45 Just beginning
47 Longtime rival of 42-Across
49 Midwest terminal?
51 Reality show documenting a two-week trade
55 "A veil, rather than a mirror," per Oscar Wilde
58 Line outside a gala
60 Dreaded message on a returned 32-Down
61 Reverse transcriptase is found in it
64 "To End ___" (1998 Richard Holbrooke best seller)
65 Q&A query
66 Barker in a basket

67 One endlessly smoothing things over?
68 Cross state

DOWN

1 Fencing material
2 Europe's City of Saints and Stones
3 Battlefield cry
4 Abstention alternative
5 "Let ___ Run Wild" (B-side to "California Girls")
6 Physical feature of Herman on "The Simpsons"
7 Home to Main Street, U.S.A.
8 The Hardy Boys and others
9 He called his critics "pusillanimous pussyfooters"

10 With flexibility in tempo
11 Reagan-___
12 Harkness Tower locale
13 Pueblo cooker
14 Red giant that disintegrated?
20 Round windows
24 Brand named after some Iowa villages
26 High (and high-priced) options for spectators
28 Rocker ___ Leo
30 Sci-fi villain ___ Fett
31 They may be made with koa wood, briefly
32 Course obstacle?
33 Elasticity studier's subj.
34 It's canalized at Interlaken
35 Boatload
37 Boatload transfer point
40 Mann's "Man!"

41 Eagle of Delight's tribe
46 Group with the 1963 hit "South Street," with "the"
48 Obsolescence
50 Moisturizer brand
52 Cry accompanying a high-five
53 Treasured strings
54 Politico caricatured by Carvey
55 Start of Egypt's official name
56 ___ Belloq, villain in "Raiders of the Lost Ark"
57 Modern farewell letters
59 Air
62 Wood problem
63 Title for knights on "Game of Thrones"

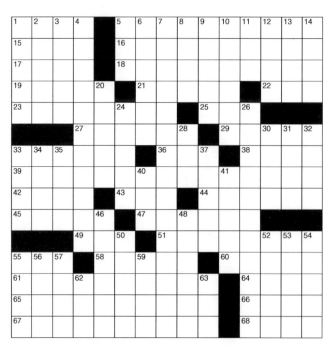

by Evan Birnholz

ACROSS

1. Neighboring
11. Far from self-effacing
15. Water-park?
16. Rose in a field
17. Singing pair
18. Old Broadway production grp.
19. Classes
20. Fresno-to-L.A. direction
21. Albuquerque's ___ Racing Museum
22. Luis who directed "Anaconda," 1997
24. Big shot on Al Jazeera
27. Passé PC piece
28. Botched
31. Oxford offering
32. Thing to charge with
36. Ghost's sound
37. Crown polisher
39. Many hand-helds, for short
40. Sleeper's option in a sleeper
41. Flee
42. Norepinephrine producer
43. Full Sail or Fuller's
44. Put on
45. Recipient of much praise
50. TALKS LIKE THIS!
52. They may sit next to castles: Abbr.
55. Aarnio of furniture
56. Oilman ___ P. Halliburton
57. Examination by those most qualified
60. GPS offerings: Abbr.
61. Old Glory saluter, most likely
62. They broke up in 1991: Abbr.
63. They're abandoned in charm school

DOWN

1. Big name in relief
2. Like wags
3. Informal name for a monkey
4. Take ___ (decline)
5. Presidential nickname
6. Accompaniers of cover letters: Abbr.
7. Basic training figs.
8. Common thing to plan a vacation around
9. Beatrix Potter's "The Tale of Mr. ___"
10. Sterile environments, for short
11. Decade or century
12. It's likely to have bass parts
13. Farthest
14. One engaging in clockwork
21. Script postscript?
23. "What ___ mind reader?"
25. "Guten ___"
26. One of the Gandhis
29. "That works"
30. Journalist who wrote "Come to Think of It," 2007
32. Contents of some music cabinets
33. Indicators of impending danger
34. Brit working with nails, say
35. Drying-out danger
36. It was retired by the Yankees in 1986
38. Powerful Syrian city in the third millennium B.C.
42. Sympathetic responses
46. 1972 Elton John hit
47. Hanover's river
48. In the back
49. Hurricane noises
51. Off, pricewise
53. It follows a mine line
54. Miss Spain, say: Abbr.
57. 43-Across server
58. That Peruvian?
59. German article

by Jim Page

ACROSS

1 1982 Stephen King horror film
10 Domain of some invasions
15 Feature of some English gardens
16 Poet who wrote "All pity is self-pity"
17 "Talk to Her" director/screenwriter, 2002
18 Papers, collectively
19 Sch. that Theo Huxtable attended on "The Cosby Show"
20 Not straight
22 Noted dark film star of the 1930s
23 Call for dinner, maybe
25 Kinda
27 Epithet for many a rapper
28 Evasive tactic
30 Classic 1977 song with the repeated line "Let's get together and feel all right"
32 ___ Lee
33 Marooned person's aid
34 Shudra, for one
37 Dungeons & Dragons figure
38 It might be cheating
39 With genuine effort
41 U.N. observer starting in '74
42 Figure of speech?
43 One of the 12 tribes of Israel
47 Moon, in Chinese
48 Arizona county with a national monument of the same name
51 Cutesy sign-off
52 Apiphobe's bane
54 Dessert with a spoon
56 Save one's breath, maybe?

57 ___-jazz
59 Queen with a prominent bust
61 "King Lear" character
62 Likely to scar
63 Crackerjack
64 It goes from post to post

DOWN

1 Political challenger's promise
2 Trust
3 "King Lear" character
4 It might get in the way of progress
5 Driver's concerns, briefly
6 Really hot
7 Retreat
8 Longtime Tanglewood figure
9 One on a lunar calendar?
10 Con target
11 Laconic
12 School
13 Annual holiday with an "airing of grievances"
14 Like a brat
21 Gender-ambiguous name
24 Cheesy crust
26 Kid-lit title character who says "I am the ruler of all that I see!"
29 Not on the level
31 "The Phantom of the Opera" writer
33 Stylish, in slang
34 Largest living rodent
35 Realized
36 Primitive

37 Like President James K. Polk
40 iPad read, maybe
41 Shape-shifting Greek sea god
44 Like a fair señorita
45 Not from around here
46 "Ain't gonna happen"
49 Former G.M. compact
50 Aladdin's enemy
53 When repeated, [Hurry it up!]
55 ". . . a man no mightier than thyself ___": "Julius Caesar"
58 Letters on some sticks
60 Pitching need

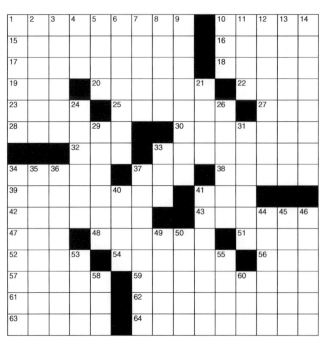

by Josh Knapp

ACROSS

1 Contemporary of Columbus
6 Stats for DVDs
10 Homey
14 Actress De La Garza of "Law & Order"
15 Latin word that's an anagram of 62-Across
16 Stone for a Libra, traditionally
17 One barely riding?
19 Put out
20 Choice for a huge movie fan?
21 20- and 60-Across, e.g.
23 Peacockery displayer
24 TravelMate notebook maker
25 Food items once called Froffles
26 Pattern seen on a diamond
30 Delay
32 Evidence of bodily harm
33 Lillie with a Tony
36 Leader in music
38 Some markets
40 Lets pass
41 All the best?
43 Husky alternatives
44 None for the money, two for the show?
46 Davis of "Bubba Ho-Tep," 2002
49 Sonoma County winery
50 First name among exotica singers
53 White alternative
55 Heart-piercing figure
56 Vulgarian
57 Summer wear for women
59 "Plaid" and "spunk" derive from it
60 ___ Blizzard (Dairy Queen offering)

61 Nonplussed
62 Be dashing
63 Keyboardist Saunders
64 Sordid

DOWN

1 Rialto setting: Abbr.
2 Crockett Hotel's neighbor
3 Malcontents
4 Stone for a Cancer, traditionally
5 Put out, in a way
6 Ready for publication
7 They cover the basics
8 Sarah Palin, self-descriptively
9 Shot
10 Wear banned in many schools
11 Impressionistic work?
12 One hard to find

13 Cagney player on TV
18 Boozing it up
22 Alternatives to Filas
27 Some bracelets
28 Almond, for one
29 What a host holds
30 Grp. operating within a network
31 Rendering on Connecticut's state quarter
33 A 1952 3-cent stamp honored her 200th birthday
34 Long reign, say
35 Numbskull
37 Minimal market purchase
39 Grant, in Glasgow
42 Pitching ace?
44 Tap add-on
45 Powerful explosive

46 Youngster with disproportionately large eyes
47 Popular vacation spot, with "the"
48 "The Liberty Bell" composer
51 Looks down
52 Try to find out what's inside
54 "___ the gods would destroy . . ."
55 Novel addendum?
58 Butt

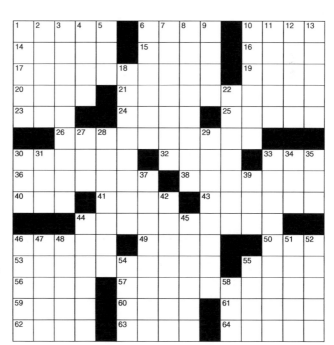

by Dana Motley

ACROSS

1 Modern drag
9 Founding need
14 It often has a crust on top
16 Visibly surprised
17 Point of no return?
18 Football Hall of Famer Bobby
19 Captain Hook's alma mater
20 "Tropic Thunder" director and co-star
22 Street heaters
25 Growth theory subj.
26 Mex. and Uru. are in it
27 "I hate this"
28 Teen series whose title character is never seen
32 Query prompted by crying
34 Turn-of-the-season mos.
35 Collusion
36 Doesn't lie gracefully
39 It set sail from Iolcus
40 Altar adjunct
41 Sole
43 Sole component
44 End for end
45 Met works
46 One way to go to a party
47 Small parts of floor plans
49 Hawks' old haunt
52 "Such mishegoss!"
53 Charged
58 Kind of mentality
59 With 61-Across, "Nothing new to me!"
60 They get picked
61 See 59-Across

DOWN

1 Web crawler
2 ___ fois que (as soon as, in Arles)
3 Chard or cab alternative
4 Defenders' assignments
5 Make some loops
6 Childish comeback
7 Item of interest?
8 Jacquet who directed "March of the Penguins"
9 Feigned incapacity
10 Even, in Évreux
11 2009 Grammy winner for "Fearless"
12 Like some sleep disruptions
13 Goats' looks
15 1990 Best Supporting Actor winner
21 Cause of a curved flight path
22 Tex-Mex topping
23 ___ Fort (World Heritage Site in India)
24 2009 comedy whose tagline is "Some guys just can't handle Vegas"
25 Yupik lang.
28 Kitten's look
29 In la-la land
30 Letters from desperate people
31 Kind of app
33 Old
36 What some gurus are called
37 She hailed from the planet Alderaan
38 Like a chorus line
40 Recreation areas: Abbr.
41 Not unless
42 1942 Preakness winner
44 Prefix with -hedron
46 It's seeing things
48 Mariposa's close relative
49 Sandwich often given a twist
50 "Ali" director Michael
51 Time for Variety?
54 Old revolutionist
55 O. T. book
56 Word after many presidents' names
57 One taking the lead?: Abbr.

by Caleb Madison

ACROSS

1 Some light fare
11 Co. now known as Ally Financial
15 Toast maker's start
16 "Streamers" playwright
17 Unlike conference games
18 Going __
19 Vision, in Vichy
20 Classic literary inits.
21 Midwestern twin city
23 Precarious positions
25 "The Gondoliers" girl
28 Poppin' Lemonade is one of its flavors
29 See 43-Across
30 Birthplace of Queen Sonja
31 Big rush
33 Where the Pawnee R. flows
35 High
37 Everywhere
41 "See ya, bro"
42 What a hand-held— or hand-holding— may be, briefly
43 With 29-Across, like many sales reps
44 Gains
46 Lake from which the Blue Nile begins
50 Motor oil letters
51 Avoid
53 Scientist for whom an element is named
54 Slugabed's state
56 Like 3 a.m., say
58 One on the Lee side?
59 Book of Mormon book
60 What you may have to enter to enter
64 Familia members
65 Almost due
66 Commune SE of Palermo
67 Is no longer fazed by

DOWN

1 Have a cold response?
2 Ricky Martin's springboard to fame
3 Big name in taco kits
4 "Give __ the play" (line from "Hamlet")
5 Old dynasty members
6 Kind of tag for a Web designer
7 One-on-one combat
8 Robert Burns's birth county
9 Suffix with proto-
10 Victors of the 1879 Battle of Isandlwana
11 Interest, informally
12 Dancer known for her execution
13 From the start
14 Air-breathing swimmer
22 1980s Cosby co-star
24 Subject of the musical "Mayor"
26 Like 24-Down, eight times
27 Causing face-clenching, maybe
30 With 62-Down, old ball game
32 Certain pancake makeup
34 Big name in skin care
36 Excites, with "up"
37 Party switcher, say
38 "Enemies, a Love Story" Oscar nominee
39 Possible response to 41-Across
40 Squirt
45 Minarets, e.g.
47 One way to study
48 Thelonious Monk's "Well You __"
49 Reflectivity measure
52 Malay for "person"
53 Places where talk is cheep?
55 Simon & Garfunkel's "El Condor __"
57 The "you" in "you will serve your brother"
61 Mercury's core?
62 See 30-Down
63 Symbol of rebellion on many T-shirts

by Tim Croce

ACROSS

1 One of the house-wives on "Desperate Housewives"
5 Spelled
15 Book with the chapter "How They Dress in Tahiti"
16 Emulated Anne Frank
17 Take one's lumps?
18 Black piecrust component
19 Conditioner's cousin
21 Mockingbird prey
22 Timon of Athens, e.g.
23 Trattoria order
24 President who won 97.6% of the vote in 2007
25 Cameo voicer on Weird Al Yankovic's "I Lost on Jeopardy"
29 Took off the table?
30 Crime lab tool
32 George III descriptor
33 "O thou pale ___ that silent shines": Burns
36 Second
37 Player who followed in Player's footsteps
38 Measure of thanks?
39 People who need to find a john?
41 Coin introduced by Louis IX
42 Word from on high
43 Ones taking off?
47 Home of the Rugby League's Rhinos
49 Quarter
50 Pursuit of Pan
51 Sensor in a CD player
55 Rock and Roll Hall of Fame doo-wop group from Baltimore
57 Backsplash piece
58 Volunteer
59 Milked

60 Obama and Clinton, for example
61 Baseball throws

DOWN

1 ___ journalism
2 Title shared by works of Ovid and D. H. Lawrence
3 Faux pas
4 Roll in a locker
5 Sporty hybrid
6 Polo of "Little Fockers"
7 Dentist's request
8 Little Thief's people
9 Relative of a carp
10 Mating call?
11 Tantalus' daughter
12 It may be assumed
13 Partner of Connecticut and Vermont

14 Starters in some fields
20 Labor group
23 Like some envelopes
25 "Home Alone" co-star
26 Texcoco denizen
27 Turn another color, say
28 Character inspired by Fu Manchu
31 So-called "Wheat Capital of the United States"
33 Frittata, e.g.
34 General Mills offering
35 University of Delaware athletes
40 Separate
44 Nancy Drew's aunt
45 Cincinnati baseballer of old

46 Stable assets
48 Family name in an 1869 romance
49 Smee and others
51 Knights' Square site
52 Myriad
53 Imperial offering
54 Jag
56 ___ Faire (re-enactors' event, informally)

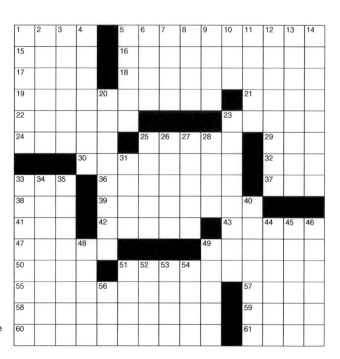

by Byron Walden

ACROSS

1 Livid
9 The "them" in "Let them eat cake"
15 Caribbean isle
16 Experts at jet propulsion
17 Colorful marine fish with spiny, fanlike fins
18 Low-scoring, as a World Cup game
19 Get a groove on?
20 Miami Heat player who was the 2006 N.B.A. Finals M.V.P.
22 "Cherry ice cream smile" wearer, in a Duran Duran hit
23 Winter Palace succession
24 Rock
25 Pacific port
27 Real-life 33-Across once played by Stallone
30 Bygone operator of N.Y.C.'s Second Avenue El
31 Org. with a "This Just In" blog
33 Person with convictions
35 Famous higher-up in admissions?
39 Departure, of a sort
40 Moderator's domain, perhaps
42 Mother of Gobo and Faline, in children's lit
43 Word of protest
44 Christie and others
46 Titan or Atlas, briefly
49 "___ Coming" (1969 hit)
51 Raw data, often
53 It makes many twists and turns
55 Admonition to one celebrating prematurely

58 Something in a crumbled state in Greece?
59 Cheer
60 Cocktail party trayful
62 Big name in fashion
63 De facto national carrier since 1932
64 Boots
65 Casino in "Casino," 1995

DOWN

1 Milk source
2 Balthasar's true identity, in Shakespeare
3 Start for Friday?
4 Practically
5 It makes mist moist
6 Coats removed before eating

7 "Atonement" novelist, 2001
8 Wanton
9 Pull up a seat for?
10 Problem to face?
11 Worries
12 Harpsichord practice piece, maybe
13 Delivery room shot
14 Without attracting attention, say
21 Stars, in a motto
23 Sacred Hindu text
26 Artist with the first hip-hop album to carry an explicit content sticker
28 Table poker?
29 Gofer's pledge
32 Extra-bright
34 Non-PC choice
35 Good thing to be on while working
36 Dr. Seuss book

37 Getting square
38 1998 De Niro film with a memorable wrong-way car chase
41 Nickelodeon's Stimpy, e.g.
45 Shrub also called meadowsweet
47 Bug
48 Hunk noted for streaking
50 About 264 gallons
52 Start of a back-up plan?
54 Goes on
56 Prophet read on Ash Wednesday
57 Middle-earth's Green Dragon and Prancing Pony
58 Classic name for a 61-Down
61 See 58-Down

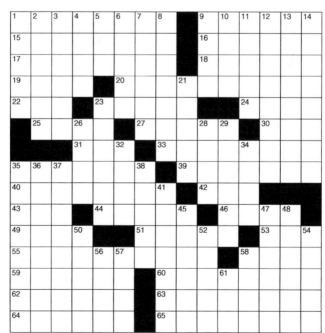

by Joon Pahk and Brad Wilber

34

ACROSS

1 "Seinfeld" holiday that begins with the Airing of Grievances
9 Uphold
15 Function-canceling setting
16 Strive to get
17 25-Across-interrupting cry
18 Fulfills a take-out order?
19 ___-voiced
20 Deep-seated
22 Old-style oath
24 See 35-Down
25 See 17-Across
28 Tag issuer, briefly
31 Women with similar habits?
34 Settings of many schools
37 One "caught" on grainy film
38 Important name in Chinese history
39 Prefix with consumer
40 Short-billed marsh bird
41 What a construction worker may bolt down
43 One whose checks should be chucked?
44 Summer threshold?
46 Literary salute
47 Naval petty officer, briefly
48 Vietnam's ___ Dinh Diem
49 Boob
52 Warehouses
54 Diners are full of them
58 Like some turkeys and geese, to cooks
61 Genre for Iggy Pop
63 Young celebrity socialite
64 Afoot
65 Holder in front of a tube
66 Many leads, ultimately

DOWN

1 Literary world traveler
2 Mindful leader?
3 ___ course
4 Section between crossbeams
5 Like some cut-rate mdse.
6 Orchestral section
7 Japanese vegetable
8 Long hauler
9 Show set in an "outer-outer borough" of New York
10 What comes out when things go up?
11 Chicken quality
12 They're unclear
13 Some eggs
14 Title box choice
21 Medium-to-poor
23 Pull funding from
25 Ingredient in colcannon, along with cabbage
26 Cut
27 Not come unglued?
28 Fancy
29 Virus or hurricane, e.g.
30 Invention inspired by burs
32 Defendant in a much-publicized 1920s trial
33 Mata ___
35 With 24-Across, bluff
36 It ended in the early 1930s
42 Way too early
45 Land near the Equator
50 Sore
51 Dodgers manager before Mattingly
52 Brouhaha
53 25-Down, informally
55 Like cut greens
56 It may be mil.
57 "___ the Limit" (Temptations album)
58 Driller
59 Safari wheels
60 Driller: Abbr.
62 Champagne article

by Kristian House

ACROSS

1 Lead
5 Intestines, e.g.
10 Dealers in books and records
14 "___ it down!"
15 Jenna Bush ___, former first daughter
16 Workers' place
17 Crush, e.g.
19 "The Gondoliers" nurse
20 Stiff
21 Like George Bush's promised nation
23 Summer mountain feature
25 "That's enough!"
27 Bill producers
28 Kind of woman
31 Explorer Amundsen
32 Spirograph, e.g.
33 Lovers of all things Barbie, say
35 Filter target
36 Odd one
39 Noted rock site: Abbr.
42 Buck for a tune?
43 Cause of a car rental surcharge
44 He was traded between Chicago teams in 1992
45 Add as a bonus
47 Some blight
49 Thick vegetable soup
52 It's a wrap
53 Like some plugs
54 Needs from
56 Tear
57 Litter, e.g.
58 Go off-shore, maybe
59 Autobús alternative
60 Like some elephants
61 CNBC subj.

DOWN

1 Visits
2 City originally known as the Town of York
3 An arm and a leg and then some
4 Keeps it coming, maybe
5 What leftovers may be for
6 Univ. aides
7 In a swivet
8 Grant
9 Anxiolytic, e.g., for short
10 Sichuan cooking ingredient
11 It may help you get a grip
12 Earl in the Baseball Hall of Fame
13 "___ me!"
18 Health products co.
22 Distended
24 Livened (up)
26 Cardinal pts.?
29 Object of some hazing
30 It's everything, it's said
33 Hits the gas
34 Taurus, for one
35 Dutch Golden Age painter
36 One who's usually gone
37 Kings and queens, say
38 Work out
39 Was given the right to vote
40 Wood lice and pill bugs
41 Starting figure on a utility bill
44 Scattered
46 ___ one (nobody)
48 Market add-on
50 Storms and others
51 What can open laterally?
53 Star of the motivational video "Be Somebody . . . or Be Somebody's Fool"
55 "Por ___ Cabeza" (tango standard)

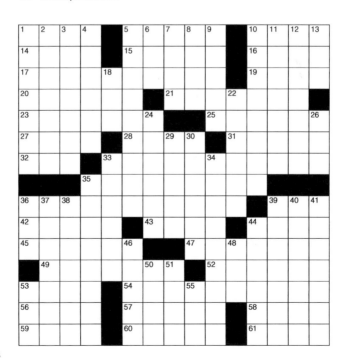

by Joe DiPietro

36

ACROSS

1 Straight person's statement
16 #1 Dire Straits hit
17 Privileged access
18 Holding heat
19 Jan ___, South African leader instrumental in establishing the League of Nations
20 South African with two U.S. Open wins
21 King with a sad end
22 Response to "Hey, I'm not perfect"
23 Sweep spots?
24 You may need to clean yours up
25 Some gowns
26 "___ me?" ("Wha?")
27 Turkey ___, slugger in the Baseball Hall of Fame
29 Like Rodin's thinker
30 Divests
31 Something to scan
32 Some dog treats
35 What fellers may be skilled with
39 Many a spring arrival
40 Need for war games
41 "Well, ___-di-dah!"
42 Big name in educational grants
43 Earl's equivalent, in Évreux
44 Shelter-providing dugout
45 Like Brahms's Piano Trio No. 1
46 Turn around on Wall Street?
47 Toughen: Var.
48 Real lowlife?
51 Schemer's quality
52 Sure things

DOWN

1 Savanna leapers
2 "Bingo!"
3 Give energy
4 Now's opposite
5 Diana with a record-setting swim around Manhattan in 1975
6 Repeatedly, in 31-Acrosses
7 They allow performers to stay on pointe
8 No great shakes
9 Afflictions of the world-weary
10 Former Senate majority leader and family
11 Posted pieces: Abbr.
12 "Bingo!"
13 Certain audio jack
14 Huddled up, e.g.
15 Expelled
22 Some are prevailing
23 Rackets
25 Exsiccates
26 Core units?
28 Cellulose fiber brand
29 Meteorological probe
31 Salsa, say
32 Option for thickening soup
33 Souter succeeded him on the Supreme Court
34 It's exploited for its crude content
35 Tiny dots on maps
36 Egg white component
37 Justify
38 Protects
40 Arrest
43 Street, in San José
44 Nero's soul
46 Not go out of service?
47 Applied sci. professional
49 Turn-of-century year
50 What April has, unlike any other month?

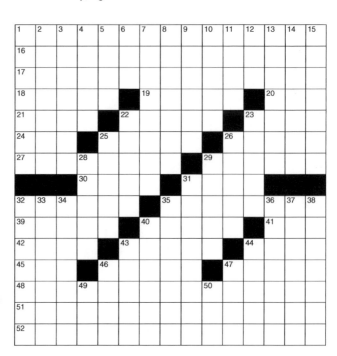

by Steve Salitan

ACROSS

1 Come to the surface
9 Place out of line
15 Light work on a stage
16 Abrupt discussion ender
17 Sci-fi vehicle
18 Bread
19 Appointed time
20 Hand helpers
22 Campaign manager?
23 Backbeat keeper
25 Early idol of Warhol
29 Pen call
30 Common menu option
33 Former big player in trading cards
34 See 46-Across
36 Skater with many trophies
37 Names on some Apple products
40 One of Ptolemy's 48 constellations
41 English philosopher Robert
42 Grunts
43 Published
45 Average name
46 With 34-Across, company's present occasion?
47 1950s "American Bandstand" dance
50 Grammy winner Adams
52 1950s living room feature
53 Scatterbrain
57 Document heading
59 Jane Goodall study site
61 1990 A.L. Rookie of the Year
62 Driving
63 Fire Chief supplier
64 Not fret

DOWN

1 Baloney
2 As far as
3 Certain squeeze
4 Chilly remark?
5 The Parisian?
6 Crude component
7 The Pioneers of the N.C.A.A.
8 Part of 37-Across's output
9 Leftover
10 Romeo's adviser, for one
11 Communal dish
12 One making a bank deposit?
13 Name on some European stamps
14 Datsun 280ZX option
21 Attempt to reach a post-departure plane?

23 Brewer Bernhard
24 Bank deposit?
25 Harp's home key
26 New model of 1999
27 Enforcer's place, often
28 Vintner's prefix
31 Samuel Johnson's only play
32 Amorous arrangement
34 Hiccup-free
35 Last name in skin care
38 Inattention indications
39 P.I.
44 Concept in Hinduism and Buddhism
46 Ancient weaponry
48 Six women at Penn programmed it
49 Not in the minority

50 No angel
51 Be the best, in slang
53 King Gorm the Old, e.g.
54 "Roll in ze hay" enthusiast in "Young Frankenstein"
55 Parents' hermanos
56 Off-the-wall
58 Balkan land, in the Olympics
60 Embarrassing eruption

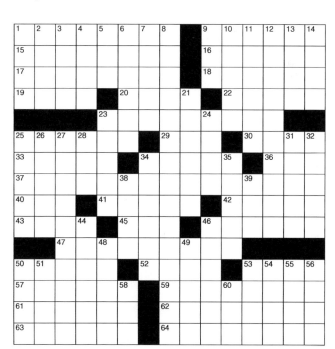

by Barry C. Silk

38

ACROSS

1 Aid in football tackling drills
9 Grifter's repertoire
14 "I'm still waiting . . ."
16 Boston pop
17 Old TV cliff-hanger
18 Jane of "Glee"
19 Little belt
20 Apple flaw
22 Pitching need
23 ___ cell
26 Recess riposte
27 Feathered 500-pounder of old
28 Unlikely ballet dancer
30 Flock member's perch
31 Turn on the waterworks
32 Epic featuring Nero
35 Corday slew him
36 Hit from Berlin
38 The Chi-___ ("Oh Girl" group)
39 Didn't change hands?
40 More than conjecture
41 Burning evidence
42 Designer of D.C.'s L'Enfant Plaza
43 "___ out!"
44 More remote
46 Auntie ___ (pretzel bakery chain)
50 Lab report?
51 Everything
53 Durham sch.
54 Big cards
56 Alfa Romeo, e.g.
59 Mammoth, old-style
60 One might go after pearls
61 Errant, to Burns
62 Port called the Cinderella of the Pacific

DOWN

1 Crowing periods
2 Square
3 One who's shortsighted
4 Treating people, briefly
5 Disdainful cry
6 Abbr. often near "R.S.V.P."
7 Bone cavities
8 "Get lost, creep!"
9 Catholic university near Tampa, Fla.
10 Hardly forward
11 "Carnival!" Tony winner Alberghetti
12 Little bit of power
13 Mush
15 E-mails, e.g.
21 Spread
24 Noisy 29-Down
25 Staples of R&B
29 See 24-Down
31 Slender brooch
32 Full of anticipation, perhaps
33 Imbecile
34 Reading for 007
35 Euripides tragedy
36 Pediatrician's amenity, often
37 React to a bad toe-stubbing
41 Holy cow for Hamburgers?
44 "___ fault"
45 He sculpted Adam and Eve
47 Milan's Porta ___
48 Finito
49 "Princess of Power" of cartoons
52 Spam is removed from them
55 Amount over due?
57 Many a paean
58 Red letters?

by Ned White

ACROSS

1 Allies who are also rivals
10 Parking permit, sometimes
15 It may be shown to a superior
16 Send out of state?
17 Ephemeral decorative structure
18 Major key that uses all five black keys on a piano
19 Fails utterly
20 "Out of Sync" autobiographer, 2007
22 "I'll be right with you"
24 First female skater to land a triple/triple jump combination in competition
25 Like some verbs: Abbr.
26 Like certain versions of the Bible: Abbr.
27 Iroquoian people
30 Means to enlightenment
31 Gets down quickly
33 ___ Diggory, rival of Harry Potter
35 Spinner's spot
38 When repeated, a Las Vegas casino
39 Five-term Mexican president
40 Gymnastics staple
41 Home of Sault Ste. Marie: Abbr.
42 Dash
44 Modern storage
47 Talking car on "Knight Rider"
49 Patch Media owner
50 Show some major respect?
53 Some magicians' gear

56 Something seen after hours?
57 Buyable, in a way
58 "Excuse me?"
60 She outwitted Sherlock
61 Major museum expense
62 Ancient manuscript
63 No longer on speaking terms

DOWN

1 Four-cornered chips
2 Make an abjuration
3 Leveled
4 Gets to first base
5 Clear
6 Cuatro semanas, roughly
7 Not domestic: Abbr.
8 Desserts not for the calorie-conscious

9 Taken care of
10 "___ Dinah" (1958 hit)
11 Like some private eyes
12 Burrito flavoring
13 British sci-fi author Reynolds
14 "It's showtime"
21 Big gigs
23 Cheek
28 What a stuck-out tongue may mean
29 Works on shifts, say
31 French horn
32 Plot devices?
34 Make the highlights?
35 2011 Wimbledon champion
36 California's ___ Serra Peak
37 Fastened tightly, with "down"

38 Refusal of Paris
40 Family of Paris
43 One bringing a speaker onstage, maybe
44 Case outcome
45 "And step on it!"
46 Got better
48 Sax great, to fans
51 Legend, for one
52 Iconic Broadway role for Cobb
54 "A Clockwork Orange" protagonist
55 Interstate hwy. ___
59 Start of many church names

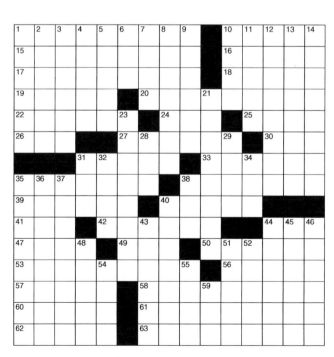

by Joon Pahk

ACROSS

1 Sarcasm indicator
10 Rating org.
14 It may give you a final answer
16 Baseball's Eddie who was nicknamed "The Walking Man"
17 Real head-turners
18 Vino place
19 Antagonistic org. in "The Simpsons Movie"
20 Speaker of the film line "This mission is too important for me to allow you to jeopardize it"
21 Libertine's opposite
23 Spanish cardinal
25 Fall sensation
27 Activity studied in onomastics
28 Currently playing
30 Brandy or whiskey
32 What a monkey may see or hear
34 "Groundhog Day" director
35 Groups of three
37 Nuclear ___
40 Discharge
42 Season finale?
44 Electrical room device
48 Probed
49 Not likely to judge
50 First of 50: Abbr.
52 Jennifer of the BBC production "Pride and Prejudice"
53 Capitol Hill sight
55 Young hunk, say
57 Cyrillic letter between kha and che
58 Desert mount
59 Union in 1999 news
62 Kind of tower
63 Modify an order?
64 Forum being
65 Is clearly #1

DOWN

1 Dean of the Truman cabinet
2 "That would be bad!"
3 Legal tender?
4 Chewable Mideast stimulant
5 Hexagon on a map
6 13th-century empire founder
7 Muse of comedy
8 Smoked delicacy
9 Slip through the cracks
10 Elvis Costello's debut album
11 Tacky yellow thing
12 Kazakhstan's capital
13 Not much, colorwise
15 Great swells
22 Showing severe erosion, maybe
24 Coin featuring a hammer and sickle
26 What may follow "NO"
29 Lead pilot's support
31 A.F.L.-C.I.O. affiliate
33 First African-American golfer to play in the Masters
36 Retired boomer
38 Like some old gaming consoles
39 Not reduced or enlarged
41 "Better Off ___" (former ABC sitcom)
43 Politico Michael and others
44 Decorated pilot
45 Ovid opus
46 Wrecks
47 1990s party name
51 Sound of silence?
54 Reduced drastically
56 Cyclops, e.g., in comic books
60 Unhelpful noughts-and-crosses line
61 ___ mission

by Milo Beckman

ACROSS

1 Facebook purchase of 2012
10 Site of the world's largest single reservoir of natural gas
15 Subject of a civil-rights investigation
16 Border
17 It might be essential
18 Old Olds
19 Datebook abbr.
20 Resourcefulness
21 Like the x- or y-axis
22 Emblem of life
24 Mad
26 Little darling
27 Pit item
29 Pay
31 "A Perfect Peace" novelist
33 It may be retracted
34 Protein powder purveyor
37 Where Wagner was born
39 Growing concern?
41 E.T.O. craft
42 First name in the Harlem Renaissance
44 Place for rods
45 Current event?
47 Skewered edible
48 Make a call to see someone nowadays?
51 It may be put on after a shower
53 TV title role for Toni Collette
54 Name on the Enterprise
55 Swarm
57 Mid first-century year
58 Avoids a service interruption
60 Climbing hazard
62 "Creation" director Jon
63 Without warning
64 Copper
65 Pint-size collectible?

DOWN

1 "Awesome party!"
2 Sing
3 Soldier on
4 Knockout number, in more ways than one
5 Have ___
6 Wood feature
7 Gaping grin
8 1997 Spielberg epic
9 ___ mal (tort reform topic, briefly)
10 "Friday Night Beauty" airer
11 Literary sextet
12 Council city of 1545–63
13 Line up
14 Primed
23 Reason for a quiet zone: Abbr.
25 Schedule
26 Breakfast fare
28 Spray source
30 Enrique Iglesias song subject
32 Kolob Arch locale
34 Refuse aid
35 L'Air du Temps perfume label
36 Singer with the double-platinum album "Measure of a Man"
38 Determination
40 Assists, say
43 France, for one
45 Shot of adrenaline?
46 Encouraging words
48 Leave in a bad place, say
49 Part of some sundae shoppe names
50 Dealer's query
52 Annual cinéma prize
56 "Meet the ___" (major-league fight song)
59 Feline
60 Chocolate ___
61 Twaddle

by David Quarfoot

42

ACROSS

1 Extension of the law?
8 Side of a diner?
14 Tragic mission
15 Jerry-built
16 First bishop of Crete, traditionally
17 Hot
18 Pioneer of slapstick cinema
19 Old means of crowd control
20 Strike out, say
21 Genesis origin?
23 Hamas rival
24 Bush cabinet member
25 Dedication, e.g.
27 Tiny carps
28 Nickelodeon's "___ Declassified School Survival Guide"
30 Last entrance to close, maybe
32 C.P.A.'s study
34 Not pummel
37 2012 honor for "4000 Miles"
41 42-Across's creator
42 Princess in 41-Across books
43 "Tepper ___ Going Out" (Calvin Trillin novel)
45 Like the army that "eagle warriors" fought in
47 Hill people
49 Feature of "pasta" and "basta"
50 Send a different way?
52 Many a bodybuilder's application
54 Born Blonde maker
55 Sleep aid
56 Like many bullies
57 Sling mud at
58 Make a connection
59 Party hearty

DOWN

1 "Mary Hartman, Mary Hartman" star
2 Agreed to take part
3 "How rude!"
4 Was fleetingly brilliant
5 Old one, in Oldenburg
6 Crushes
7 He supplied Lex Luthor with red kryptonite
8 Birth year of King Philip I
9 Not less than
10 "The Bartered Bride" composer
11 Joined the fight
12 School
13 They're plumbed
15 Case for a psychoanalyst
22 Adventurer Casanova
26 Not go on
29 Bullet-catching place?: Abbr.
31 Storm producer, once
33 Largest active volcano in Japan
34 Fast, graceful runner
35 Mouth of a river
36 Like some professors
38 Ancient double-deckers
39 Query upon witnessing a hanging?
40 How hordes advance
41 Where to get loaded after loading
44 Crude vessel
46 Stone unit
48 O.K.
51 King of verse
53 Zouave headgear

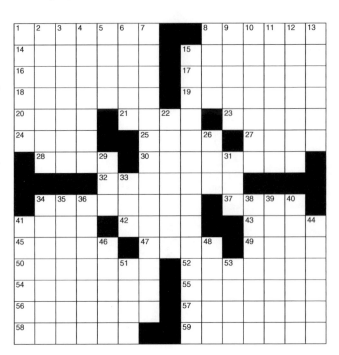

by Tim Croce

ACROSS

1 Shaggy dog
7 It's gone over with poles
14 African country with a namesake lake
15 Rival of Paris
17 Contemptuously bold
18 Self-doubting
19 Extra desire?
20 Prefix with -zoic
22 O.K. for another season
23 Stop going
24 "Fiddlesticks!"
25 Eastern melody
26 Like many a romance hero
28 Raiders org.?
31 Call __
32 Secret weapon
35 1978 sequel set in a shopping mall
37 It might pop up at a nursery
38 Crumb
39 These, in Toulon
40 Charge
44 Far from whole
46 Like refreshing agua
47 Fellow in a counting-out rhyme?
48 Senator of Watergate fame
50 "South Park" co-creator Stone
51 Hustle
52 Like four ill-fated popes, it's said
54 Spike
56 Where things might pop up in a nursery
57 He took Rehnquist's seat
58 Home of Mandalay
59 Ones given money to waste?

DOWN

1 Showed no hurry in getting somewhere
2 Breakfast bowlful
3 The endocrine system, essentially
4 Break a pledge?
5 State at a spectacle
6 It might be hard-pressed to get assistance
7 Expert on forgery?
8 Vegas game
9 Hookups
10 Razz
11 Inside trouble
12 Peak east of Captain Cook
13 Killer source material for a comedian, say
16 Pollution concern
21 Invitation stipulation
24 It might be put on a blanket
27 Atlanta cager
28 Fundamentally
29 Who "are coming," in a historical declaration
30 Part of a Freddy Krueger costume
33 Math ordinal
34 One meter start?
35 Developing area
36 Goings-on
37 Patron saint of the Catholic Church
41 Response to "Don't panic!"
42 Hands-on position?
43 Like the beast in Hercules' first labor
45 Diminutive for Baryshnikov
46 Radio knob
49 Showdown time
50 Southwest city founded by Mormon pioneers
51 Run-in
53 Book before Deut.
55 Old long-distance letters

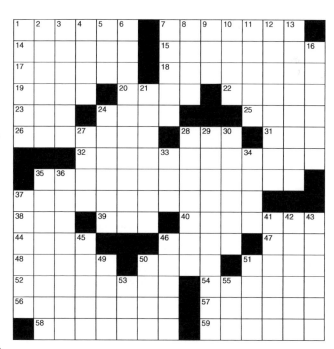

by Josh Knapp

ACROSS

1 What many a character in "The Iceman Cometh" expresses
10 Part of a Spanish forest
15 1997 voice role for Meg Ryan
16 It's in front of a benched player
17 It may be replaced by a dash
18 Corny fare?
19 Second-largest moon in the solar system
20 Month before Tishri
22 Astronomer's calculation: Abbr.
23 Lab directive?
24 Desert gullies
26 Letter after Oscar
27 The dark side
28 Happens to
30 Italian almond cookies
35 Put more layers on
36 Tremendously
38 Where blackbirds may be baked?
39 Poses a bomb threat?
40 Emulated Tiresias
42 Realize
43 Texter's "bye now"
44 All ___ (store sign)
46 "Every saint has a ___": Oscar Wilde
50 Magic, on scoreboards
51 Subject of King Deioces
52 Eponymous container
53 National Voting Rights Museum locale
55 Virginia v. Sebelius subject, in headlines
58 Accord

59 Prominently demonstrated
60 Binary, in a way
61 1999 Best Director winner

DOWN

1 Accords
2 Certain harpooner
3 First section
4 Locke work
5 Decahedron-shaped die, to a gamer
6 Still green, or still red
7 That, in Toledo
8 Ran
9 Fill-in-the-blank story
10 Washer, e.g.: Abbr.
11 2014 World Cup locale, for short
12 India's so-called "Garden City"
13 It's beside the point

14 Got older and slower
21 Paywall charges
24 Effortlessly
25 Like con men?
26 Betrayed anxiety, say
27 Beasts of the East
29 "1234" singer, 2007
30 Seemingly expressing
31 Egg-laying mammal
32 Belladonna lily
33 What like charges do
34 Dutch financial giant
37 No longer to be found
41 ___ walk (old house feature)
45 "I finally got around to reading the dictionary. Turns out the ___ did it": Steven Wright
46 Tough nut to crack

47 Court determination
48 Certain noncom
49 They may be clear-cut
51 Bread spread
52 Lowland
54 High point: Abbr.
56 Direct
57 "Hill Street Blues" production co.

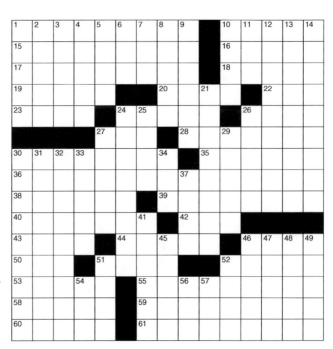

by Joon Pahk

ACROSS

1 A flat alternative
7 Like some alibis and stomachs
15 Green wheels
16 Oscar-nominated player of Sonny Wortzik
17 Salsa brand
18 Telephone connectors
19 One for the team?
20 Better
22 Fig. on some applications
23 1935 Cagney crime film
25 Rich sources of vitamin K
26 Diamond with many cuts
27 "Use ta Be My Girl" group, with "the"
29 They're crunchable: Abbr.
30 Seminal name in science fiction
31 Mr. Pricklepants in "Toy Story 3," e.g.
33 How many are chosen?
34 Pentateuch peak
35 Least legitimate
39 Rich or poor: Abbr.
40 Its members are in order
41 Toolbar lineup
44 Going rate?: Abbr.
45 Deadening device
46 Experience ecdysis
47 One of the Jonas brothers
49 "Dracula" heroine Harker
50 Series after the opener?
51 Wings
53 Unpleasant sound in nature
54 Woman who's hard to reach

56 Seat of New York's Chemung County
58 Part of many a detour
59 "Fudge!"
60 Like some martinis
61 Beer hall turn-on?

DOWN

1 German resistance leader?
2 Boeing X-51 engine, e.g.
3 They snap easily
4 One in play?
5 Frequent feeling for 3-Down
6 Shoe-lacing, e.g.
7 Made-to-order item?
8 Wear with flares
9 Processor speed, hard disk space, etc.

10 It's often handed down
11 Where you may be in France
12 Player who's way too good, say
13 Part of a lane arrangement
14 Deal-killing declaration
21 Bank of ___ (institution the A-Team was jailed for robbing)
24 Big Blue member, for short
26 Washington attraction with a punny name
28 Radios, e.g.
30 Soft palate
32 Fifth pillar of Islam
33 Newbie's resource

35 Cartoon character that was one of the first images transmitted on TV
36 Like sirens
37 Novel creation
38 A whole lot of juice?
40 Ytterbium's atomic number
41 Tipple
42 Sacrum neighbor
43 Senior
44 Front
47 Hit below the belt
48 Calls for
51 Mystique
52 "How dare you!" accompanier
55 One ends on Sept. 30
57 Anatomy test, briefly?

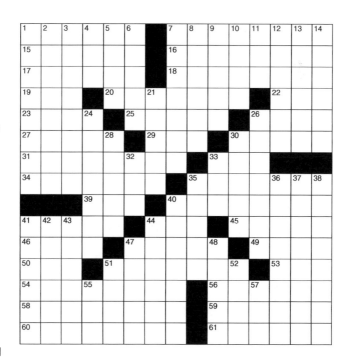

by Barry C. Silk

46

ACROSS

1 Java application?
12 E-mails a dupe
15 Swearing-in figure
16 Onetime giant in decking
17 Raphael, e.g.
18 It may have no stars
19 Film producer Fayed
20 Birthplace of the phonograph
22 Ruling group
23 Heads across the pond
25 Standing by
26 Cold front?
27 Gran Paradiso, e.g.
29 Prepares to be discharged
31 It goes over the tongue
34 Guitar-spinning group
35 City of a quarter million founded on a ranch site
37 ___ fit
38 Shred
39 Prefix with Germanic
40 Three-sided carrier
41 Peak periods
42 Piña colada topping?
44 Web site crasher?
45 M quarter
48 Specifically
51 Composer Siegmeister
52 Greetings
53 Bit of ancient art
56 ___ polar (animal del Artico)
57 Singer who founded Righteous Babe Records
58 Victor over H.H.H.
59 It competed with Mail Boxes Etc.

DOWN

1 Origin of the word "cheetah"
2 F-, for one
3 Secures
4 It blew in 1707
5 Ottoman dignitary
6 Real fan
7 Makeup of some kits
8 Storied slacker
9 Routing abbr.
10 Move with a bobbing motion
11 Common cooler
12 Charge storer
13 Home of Pomona College
14 Settle
21 Big squares
23 Overgrown, say
24 Mobile
26 Wii, for one
27 Nose-burning
28 One may be taken in faith
30 Facial site
31 Its central deity is Amaterasu
32 Claims
33 Like sports cars, briefly
34 Full of energy
35 Eastern energy
36 1980s Argentine president Alfonsín
40 Hydrocarbon in gasoline
43 1-Across may be added to it
44 Neighbor of McGuire A.F.B.
45 Can
46 A third of quince
47 Toy snappers
48 Dweller in the hall Bilskirnir
49 Like a 6-Down
50 Turn over
51 Actor McGregor
54 N.Y.C.'s ___ Bridge
55 Talent agent Emanuel

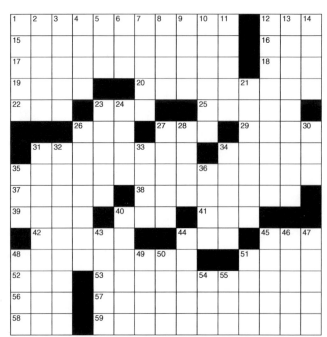

by Will Nediger

ACROSS

1 Giving a wide berth
16 What an environmentalist wants to reduce
17 "My mistake"
18 What instrumentalists often change
19 7-Down's goals, briefly
20 Set up: Abbr.
21 She, in Lisbon
22 "According to old wisdom . . ."
34 Something passed on the way to court?
35 Singer of the 2010 #1 hit "Rude Boy"
36 Post-winter breakup
37 Anguished
38 Like a bugbear
40 End a split
41 Its first C.E.O. was the W.W. I hero Eddie Rickenbacker
43 Big check-printing co.
44 Not flee
48 "___ true"
49 Car ad fig.
53 FEMA mission
57 One whose goal is changing shape?
58 Info on a medical history form

DOWN

1 Med., e.g.
2 Unpleasant thing to be taken to
3 "Broadway's in Fashion" artist
4 Owner of Bill Me Later
5 Running back Dayne and others
6 Birthplace of Rex Stout and Kurt Vonnegut: Abbr.
7 Bears, e.g.
8 Substantial
9 Pirate
10 It's often 11 in. long
11 French-derived word with two accents
12 Fly balls, e.g.
13 "Hud" director
14 Going along the line, briefly?
15 1-800-SEND ___ (apropos corp. number)
22 Brook
23 Vertebral column parts
24 Almonds and pistachios
25 Afghan province or its capital
26 Radiate
27 Less likely to crack
28 Pyrotechnics compound
29 One present in spirit?
30 Adorned, on menus
31 Odds opener
32 Maternally related
33 Is enough for
39 Common cold case reviver
40 Comeback
42 Fan
44 Set on the Saône?
45 On deck, say
46 Lloyd in the College Football Hall of Fame
47 Ending with fluor-
49 Trailer-approving grp.
50 Meat sticker
51 Pasta ___ (Quaker brand)
52 Before: Abbr.
53 Place for a trophy case
54 "___ true"
55 Surfer's address
56 30% of dieci

by Tim Croce

ACROSS

1 Urban contemporary
6 "Git!"
11 Sports org. of 1967–76
14 Olive-colored bird
15 World powerhouse in table tennis
16 Word of logic
17 Bygone theory of astronomy
20 Blanket
21 Round parts
22 Hideous one
26 Get-___ (starts)
29 Obituary word
30 Bugs
33 "Ugly Betty" actress
39 Governor, e.g.
40 "Idylls of the King," stylistically
41 1959 doo-wop classic
42 Alpine native
43 "Grazie ___!" (Italian for "Thank God!")
44 Basketball Hall-of-Famer Dan
45 Thrust item
48 Uses for a base
50 Balderdash
54 E.E.C. part: Abbr.
55 It may be bitter
56 "I did it!"
57 Grp. in gray
58 Gridiron distance: Abbr.
59 Sporting boots, say

DOWN

1 Tube rating
2 It may be performed by people in robes
3 Unyielding
4 Part of 1-Down
5 "___ is human . . ."
6 It has thousands of roots

7 Half of a classic religious symbol
8 ___-A-Che (rapper)
9 Response: Abbr.
10 Wishy-washy reply
11 Deal preceder
12 Participant in an 1899 conflict
13 ___ deal
18 Risqué West
19 Ones to whom an organization's messages are sent
23 Frayed, perhaps
24 Funny Carol and family
25 "Woe is me!" types
26 Land visited by Paul in the New Testament

27 Clarinet need
28 Concealments
31 "I'll be right with you"
32 Elided phrase in a Gershwin song
33 Easily corrupted
34 One-seat carriages
35 Assailed
36 Verona's river
37 They have their pride
38 More crafty
46 Certain bird herd
47 Per
48 Wished otherwise
49 Supporter of the Heller decision, 2008: Abbr.

50 Allergy source
51 Played out
52 Abbr. after a telephone no.
53 One with two or three stripes: Abbr.

by Joe Krozel

ACROSS

1 Reconcile
10 Certain Arabian Peninsula native
15 Nancy Pelosi's Emmy-nominated daughter
16 Test for a tailor
17 Mork first appeared on it
18 Boot
19 Cons
20 Graceful genie of myth
22 See 50-Across
23 Interrogee, often
24 "Crimes of Passion" Grammy winner
27 Bone: Prefix
28 Price of music
29 Guinier of civil rights
30 City of 750,000 SW of Warsaw
31 Big name in car batteries
32 Drummer with a star on the Walk of Fame
38 Time release
39 Kind of surgery
40 Where Wyatt Earp operated the Dexter Saloon
41 G follower
43 Urgent alerts, briefly
47 It may be followed by [sic]
49 Onetime big name in hair removal
50 Opposites of 22-Acrosses
51 What birds take
52 First name in 1950s politics
53 1998–2007 Lebanese president Lahoud
55 It doesn't include a bass

58 Hit most likely to start an unassisted triple play
59 Miss in an aisle
60 Symbols of industry
61 The Marx Brothers in "Monkey Business," e.g.

DOWN

1 "___ nui loa" (Hawaiian words of gratitude)
2 Self-titled debut album of 1991
3 Didn't stop
4 Run out
5 With 35-Down, joins the club, perhaps
6 Shut off
7 Novelist Leverson
8 Sasquatch studier, say
9 Slip past
10 Didn't run out for dinner
11 Philly court legend
12 Shrimp protrusion
13 "Never"
14 Kind of paint
21 Word with cent or cell
24 Blizzard battler
25 Designer Gucci
26 Writer Wilkinson of The New Yorker
30 Cleaning agent
31 Atl. Coast state
32 Big name in gossip, once
33 Basis of the song "It's Now or Never"
34 Dialyzing
35 See 5-Down
36 "Doggone!"
37 Crown

41 E.P.A. computation
42 Tinactin target
43 Merry-___ (clown)
44 Jai alai need
45 Knockout
46 Frond supporters
48 They hold water
52 Noted Indian burial site
54 Constellation that looks like a bent coat hanger
56 Density symbol
57 Tennis's Hoad

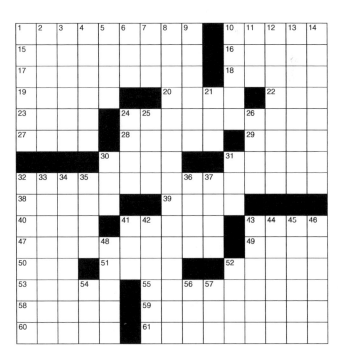

by Barry C. Silk

50

ACROSS

1 Birder's reward
9 Amount of olives
15 Not nervous at all
17 They might make a dog run
18 On-air hobbyists?
19 Inspire warm feelings about
20 Aristotle's "___ Rhetorica"
21 Select
23 Suffix with cannon
24 Oil deposit problem
25 Sports org. with the Colorado Rapids
26 Jester's locale
29 Shortbread flavorer
30 Much paperwork
31 Be in the can
32 "If you can find a better car, buy it" pitchman
35 Like some fake redheads
36 "___ Heart" (1988 Whoopi Goldberg film)
37 Fit for the road, say
38 Promising location
39 ___ macchiato
40 "Deo vindice" was its motto: Abbr.
43 In the wrong business?
44 Litter critter
45 Ooh and aah, e.g.
47 Big 12 sch.
48 Emulates Chicken Little
51 Pico Mountain innovation of 1940
52 1992 chick-lit best seller set in Phoenix
55 "Different strokes for different folks"
56 Like many measuring spoons
57 Air

DOWN

1 Algonquian chief
2 Promising start?
3 One of Macbeth's thanedoms
4 Jack or forklift
5 Exaggerated workload
6 Key
7 Foreign refusal
8 Look-sees
9 "Aladdin" villain
10 Smoking, say
11 Wood or Underwood
12 Thick base for pizza
13 Connection requirement, at times
14 Fell off
16 Activity with traps
22 Green jam ingredient?
24 Fortune 100 company named after a smoker
27 "The Two Towers" army
28 Portrayer of June in "Henry & June"
29 Weigh
30 Venture
31 Dimple
32 Sad sack's lament
33 Earmark
34 Wear for some superheroines
35 Like chop-shop cars
37 Element
39 Pair in a cage
40 Place to change trunks
41 Barista's injuries
42 Stationary
44 Did a rush job on?
46 Code of conduct
48 Anti-cavalry weapon
49 ___ Hamels, 2008 World Series M.V.P.
50 Move through a market
53 Body image, briefly
54 Vintage Jaguar

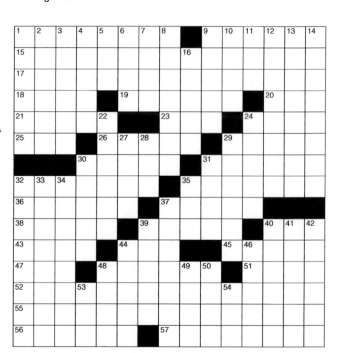

by Doug Peterson and Brad Wilber

ACROSS

1 Religious emblem, informally
10 Jerks
15 "Il dolce suono," e.g.
16 It's worth 8 points in English and 10 points in French
17 Backwater, in Australia
18 Certain pub
19 GPS heading
20 A search may be done with it
21 Fluff
22 Figure on a table: Abbr.
24 Works in a studio, say
26 Schubert piece
27 Get along
29 Reason to end an engagement
31 Virus containment specialist
33 List
34 Alpine stream
35 You can feel it on the ground, informally
37 Girl's name that becomes a boy's name when the last letter moves to the start
39 Envelope abbr.
42 Lump
44 Market
48 Guitar device producing a vibrato effect
51 Beat
52 Chilling
53 On a list of knowns
55 Filled
56 Ages
57 Roast setting
59 Travel ___
60 Orkney Islands clan
62 Needlework?
64 Dioxane, e.g.
65 Measure of progress
66 Hyundai model
67 So simple

DOWN

1 Governmental stimulus of 2012
2 Missive
3 Kind of acid that dissolves gold
4 It might be a link
5 Auto with a "9" in almost all its model names
6 Onetime spokesmodel for I Can't Believe It's Not Butter
7 Having a twist
8 Grappler's gear
9 No beauty
10 Rose on stage
11 Carleton College rival
12 Mediterraneo tourist locale
13 Hyundai model
14 Fizz
23 A power of dos
25 Breeze (through)
26 Post-cookout item
28 Cry when reaching the other side
30 Hunk
32 Tough to grasp
36 "Place without water," in Mongolian
38 Shade on the Riviera
39 Comics character named for a flower
40 High-end accommodations, familiarly
41 Otalgia
43 Statistician's anathema
45 Opening words deliverer
46 What goes before that goes?
47 Period of radio silence
49 Buddy
50 Some western gear
54 Jingle, e.g.
58 Introductory course?
61 Sp. name preceder
62 Japanese market inits.
63 Sweet ending?

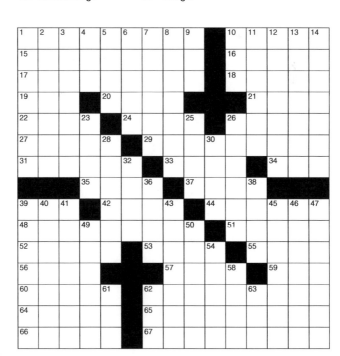

by David Quarfoot

52

ACROSS

1 Rainbow event
10 Given orally, at law
15 Maureen of "Tarzan the Ape Man"
16 Russian princess who was Nicholas II's only niece
17 One of a chain owned by Wyndham
18 Platte River natives
19 "Unfaithful" Oscar nominee
20 See 26-Across
21 "Come on down!" announcer
22 Ode title opener
23 Receipt to redeem a credit
24 Place of imprisonment in book and film
26 With 20-Across, Conan's domain
27 Worried about, in slang
32 What repeats in solemn hymns but isn't in hymnals?
34 One who snaps
35 First-ever
36 "Indeed, mate"
38 Shaking
39 Pianist Gilels
40 Prepare for a long drive
42 Falls off
44 Maxwell rival
45 "The strain seemed doubly dear, / Yet ___ sweet": Wordsworth
50 Butler who played Grace Kelly
51 Setting for the swing set?
53 Thor's group

54 She told Willy Wonka "Loompaland? There's no such place"
55 Signs of spring
56 Clear thinker's asset
57 American tribe that lent its name to a state
58 Non-profit concerns?

DOWN

1 Monkey launched into space in 1958
2 Repeated cry from Mercutio in "Romeo and Juliet"
3 Arizona natives
4 City whose name is Spanish for "flat"
5 Mayflower man
6 100 fils
7 Winged it?
8 Activia maker
9 Standard sudoku groupings, e.g.
10 No-spin particles
11 It includes the extradition clause
12 It's between Laredo and Nuevo Laredo
13 Performance with nearly perfect pitch?
14 What a broke person is down to
24 Feeling no physical attraction?
25 Prepare to fire into the sky
27 Kind of earring requiring twisting
28 1919–33, in German history
29 Pre-takeoff command

30 One side in the Bay Bridge Series rivalry
31 Southeast Asian observance
33 Medieval love poem
37 Mae West reputedly said this "is good to find"
38 Military hut
41 Aspartame developer
43 Tiny groove
45 Ensure
46 Sounds that make frogs disappear?
47 "Jezebel" star
48 Coeur d'___
49 They go down when it's cold
52 ___-C

by Raymond C. Young

ACROSS

1 HanesBrands brand
8 Exercise in a pool
14 General goal?
15 Tribe whose name means "those with many tattoos"
17 Feeler, of sorts
18 Title under which "The Lion Sleeps Tonight" originally charted, in 1952
19 Name for the T. rex at Chicago's Field Museum
20 23-Across's target reader
22 Chaps
23 Bygone 20-Across fashion magazine
25 Musical intensifier
28 Mythical predator of elephants
29 Numerical prefix
33 Stations
34 Highway sections
36 Skating gold medalist of 1928, 1932 and 1936
37 Figure in a beret
38 ___ Derby, annual sporting event since 1866
39 Grub sellers
41 ___ Park
42 Geneva-based org. encouraging healthy living
43 One of 100 in un siglo
44 Word appearing 39 times in the King James Version of Matthew 1
45 Composure
49 Genre of the double platinum box set "Songs of Freedom"
52 One going to court?

53 Utmost
56 Post, e.g.
58 Napping
60 Job-like
61 City where Jonah preached
62 Cote d'Azur town
63 Nightwear

DOWN

1 E-1s and E-2s, in the Army: Abbr.
2 Place
3 High-school spots?
4 Financial statement abbr.
5 They bite but don't have teeth
6 Great Lakes natives
7 Upward-flowing plant vessels
8 Black bird
9 Pore, e.g.

10 Popular Debussy piece
11 Fictional boxer a k a The Count of Monte Fisto
12 Machine part connecting to a gearwheel
13 New York Jets home from 1964 to 1983
16 Quizzical cries
21 Top of the charts?
23 Amount of appreciation, maybe
24 Is piercing
25 "Shampoo" director
26 Tick off
27 Sega mascot
30 "I ___"
31 Unit of magnetic flux density
32 Have ___ at
34 Latte go-with

35 Hip-hop producer for Jay-Z, LL Cool J and Missy Elliott
40 "Try it!"
46 Not left over
47 Frequent
48 "Journey to ___" (recurring "Sesame Street" segment)
49 Criticize
50 "M*A*S*H" maneuver, for short
51 Bhagavad ___ (Hindu scripture)
53 Riders on Direhorses in "Avatar"
54 Certain diagram
55 Little chortles
57 Some football linemen: Abbr.
59 Jump the broom, so to speak

by Gareth Bain

ACROSS

1 Setting for part of "A Tale of Two Cities"
9 "Awww!"
15 Aces, with "the"
16 What a mass of footballers do after a tackle
17 One getting poked in the eye?
18 Smell like
19 Punches, informally
20 Psychologist Alfred
21 Jaunty
23 Not taking a loss well, say
24 High, in a way
25 Its positions are labeled North, South, East and West
29 Number of Planeten
30 Ones who are counter-productive?
32 Funny Margaret
33 Completely covers
34 Nag (at)
35 Microwaveable food brand
37 Centimeter-gram-second unit
38 Dead duck, maybe
39 Union V.I.P.
40 One might be performed en avant
41 Grow more and more irksome
42 Country music's Carter
44 Architectural base
46 Film hero chasing a motorcycle gang
47 Put on the line
50 "Let's do it!"
51 Chatted up
52 ___ Puffs
53 Target of thrown bricks, in early comics

DOWN

1 N.C.A.A. football ranking system
2 "Now I see!"
3 Picture on file
4 "The Hippopotamus" writer
5 "Wait, this isn't making sense"
6 Separate through percolation
7 Sure thing
8 Milk sources
9 Concorde features
10 Rare driving choices
11 Like some flexible mortgages
12 Exercise ___
13 Loads
14 "___ Poetry Jam"
21 Raid target
22 Position in a relay
23 Historical community
25 Rap's Biz ___
26 Last name in women's skin care
27 "Pretty obvious, huh?"
28 Certain coffee order
30 I.R.S. settlement
31 Take turns?
33 Part of a cover
36 Some silk threads
37 Trounce
39 Cuban-born Baseball Hall-of-Famer José
41 Terra ___
42 "Baa, Baa, Black Sheep" figure
43 Threshold
44 Load
45 One who's incredible
46 Peace abroad
48 Listing that can change based on the weather, for short
49 Flyspeck

by Peter Wentz

ACROSS

1 Help for someone just browsing?
8 1-Across source
15 Raving
16 Buds
17 Stimulant
18 "The Consul" composer
19 What a screen may block
21 Submitted
22 Noggins
24 Mouth filler
25 Zulu's counterpart
29 "___Arizona Skies" (early John Wayne film)
31 Giveaway
33 Stimulate
35 Shadows
37 Creature whose genus name and English name are the same
38 Dare to put in one's two cents
41 Tool shed tool
42 Flip
43 Clipped
44 Number of strings on a Spanish guitar
46 Tourney round
48 Some homages
49 Bush whackers?
51 Actress Berger
53 Not strictly adhering to tempo
55 Part of an ice pack?
59 Simian
61 Series begun in 2007
63 Bet everything
64 Midday appointments
65 Like some director's cuts
66 Wraps

DOWN

1 Goliath, e.g.
2 "Suicide Blonde" band
3 Torment
4 ___Railroad, 1832–1960
5 Like a lot?
6 Shipping weight
7 They might include BMX and wakeboarding, informally
8 Year "Tosca" premiered
9 Sources of iron and manganese
10 Defensive strategies
11 Part of a plot
12 Source of a secret, in a phrase
13 Triple-platinum Gloria Estefan album with "Rhythm Is Gonna Get You"
14 Alphabet book phrase
20 Spies often don't use them
23 Queued
25 Eastern generals
26 Stockpiled
27 Orange children's character
28 Actor Butterfield of "Hugo"
30 Fielder's challenge
32 Pool parts
34 Bit of work
36 Alma mater for McDonnell and Douglas of McDonnell Douglas
39 Bashes
40 Prefix with realism
45 Part of an "@" symbol
47 Board
50 Supporting post
52 Temporarily formed
53 ___Bolognese
54 Sooner alternative
56 Spanish title
57 "Your" alternative
58 "Days of Heaven" co-star, 1978
60 Wideout, in football
62 Stovetop sound

by Michael Ashley

56

ACROSS

1 Dragging vehicles
10 Massachusetts governor after John Hancock
12 One who was very successful with numbered balls
14 Advance man?
15 Some clouds
17 Cerebral canals
18 Crook's mark
21 Apostle of Ire.
22 Plate setting
23 Board game found in Egyptian tombs
25 Group led by a Grand Exalted Ruler
26 "The Chronicles of Vladimir ___" (hit young adult book series about a vampire)
27 Feature of some televised debates
29 Spanish demonstrative
30 Long and twisty
31 "The L Word" network, in listings
32 Survey militarily
34 Canvas in a wooden frame, of sorts
35 Yeomen of the Guard officer
36 Ready to play
37 Number one, to some
38 Old letters
40 "Combats avec ___ défenseurs!" (line from "La Marseillaise")
41 In a way, informally
42 Some Japanese-Americans
44 Period of slow growth
45 One who is very successful with numbered balls

49 One getting laughs at others' expense
50 Exercise leader

DOWN

1 Stopped flowing
2 Exeunt ___ (stage direction)
3 Violin virtuoso Leopold
4 French preposition
5 Street caution
6 Part of an equitable trade, figuratively speaking
7 Writer LeShan and others
8 Bundles of logs, maybe
9 Not so dim
10 Dublin-born singer with a 1990 #1 hit
11 Kings' home
12 GQ sort of guy
13 Part-owner, say
14 Mess makers
16 "Just a few more miles"
18 Hit show
19 Chemical used in dyes
20 Dress store section
23 Weary
24 Reproved, in a way
27 Sessions in D.C., say
28 Battle of ___ (first Allied victory of W.W. I)
33 Like some shopping
37 Luster, e.g.
39 Gripping parts of gecko footpads
41 "Roots" family surname
43 Superlative suffix
44 ___ list
46 Map abbr.
47 Soprano Sumac
48 Mil. branch disbanded in 1978

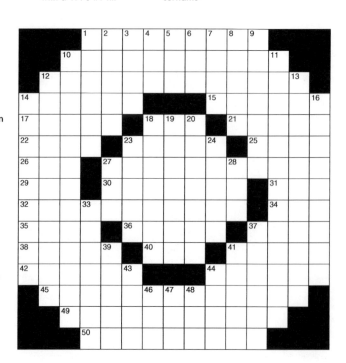

by Todd Gross

ACROSS

1 White-whiskered sort
10 Symbol of Einstein's gravitational constant
15 Eager
16 Tons
17 Time of one's life
18 Youngest of five famous brothers
19 Ernst associate
20 Things worth waiting for?
21 What head shots are used in
22 People pick pockets in it
23 Eddie's partner in musical comedy
24 Burial option
25 Cut out for it
28 Intentionally flooded field
30 Short order?
31 One working with magnetite
33 Minor, legally
35 "Ha! Good one!"
37 "Bummer"
38 Word below a signature on a bill
39 Zero, in 21-Across
40 They often have good rhythm
41 Mr. T's real last name
42 Julia Child worked for it during W.W. II: Abbr.
43 Lav
44 Escalator pioneer
46 Fox on Fox
48 Blast alternative?
49 Traffic court letters
52 Facilitators of cultural growth
53 Toxicodendron diversilobum
55 Yogi Bear co-creator

56 Off-roading option
57 Fire
58 Grocery product with green leaves in its logo

DOWN

1 400-pound calf, perhaps
2 Player of a big scaredy-cat?
3 No Mr. Personality
4 Drug czar Kerlikowske
5 Put an ___
6 Where the Blue Nile rises
7 Jellyfish and krill
8 Some are fragile
9 Bygone means of corporal punishment
10 Buzz generator

11 "I'll Be Around" songwriter Wilder
12 TV Guide crossword focus
13 Something that shouldn't scare you
14 Garnish
21 Arch
22 Marker maker
23 It features a statue of a Scottie next to his master
25 Title slave of the stage
26 First cut on the album "Sticky Fingers"
27 Home of the Ducks of baseball's Atlantic League
29 Handle on farm equipment?
30 Humdingers
32 Fr. address

33 Texting counterpart of "TY"
34 Sno-___ (winter blower brand)
36 Orwellian superstate
40 One of nine numbers on a card
42 Clarkson College locale
43 Alpo alternative
45 "___ you!"
47 1958 spy novel set in Jamaica
48 "Cannery Row" brothel owner
49 "Get busy!"
50 Boat trailer?
51 Pottery Barn competitor
53 54-Down tally: Abbr.
54 See 53-Down: Abbr.

by Barry C. Silk

ACROSS

1 "8mm" star, 1999
12 "Applesauce!"
15 It has a Snapshot Tool command
16 Irish ___
17 His 1978 album "Excitable Boy" went platinum
18 Marathoner Pippig
19 Mrs. Gorbachev
20 Bicycle support, informally
22 1956 Santos rookie
23 Groupie's trait
25 Past-tense verb that is the same as its present-tense form minus the fourth and fifth letters
26 Jane who was Chicago's first female mayor
28 Title science teacher of an old sitcom
31 Mud
32 Place for locks and pins
34 ___fide
35 Gets in a lather
37 Won't allow
41 Mrs. Grundy type
43 Far East capital
44 Kind of root in math
45 Milk producer
49 Circus Maximus stars?
51 Soviet attack sub
52 Gardener's purchase
54 Bait thrown overboard
55 Wine-tasting accessory
58 Pair in an average-sized orchestra
60 Get an edge on?
61 One stoked to provide warmth
64 A simpler one may be recalled
65 Black-and-white, say
66 Typical house on "Hoarders"
67 Flashlight alternatives

DOWN

1 Sticks nix
2 "Go ahead and try!"
3 Orange relative
4 Inner Party member in "1984"
5 Sake brewery byproduct
6 Star with two stars on the Hollywood Walk of Fame
7 Informal remarks?
8 Image on a denarius
9 Sominex alternative
10 Storms, e.g.
11 Cousins of kites
12 Bagatelle
13 Pioneering microcomputer
14 Rakes often break them
21 Shrilly talk to
22 Many tykes' lunches
24 Potential throat clearer, briefly
27 Filing aid
29 Hangover?
30 Justice Kagan
33 "Highly doubtful"
36 Baltic Sea swimmer
38 Live, maybe
39 Ancient dweller in the Po Valley
40 Comforter go-with
42 Lugs
43 First name on the 1954 album "Mambo!"
45 Five of them represent a zero
46 The "A" of A&M Records
47 Polite cut-in
48 Chaucer's "Merciless Beauty," e.g.
50 Its contents are often wicked
53 Be a blessed person, per Matthew 5:4
56 Skinny-minny
57 Princess in Donald Duck cartoons
59 Certain pack member
62 Abbey title
63 They have high stations

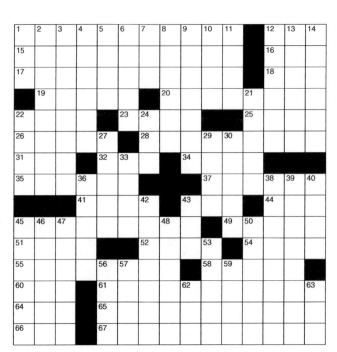

by David Steinberg and Barry C. Silk

ACROSS

1 Increases the intensity
10 High-hatter's wear?
15 Totally plugged-in
16 Bury
17 Sheepskin source
18 Spirit, in Stuttgart
19 Maximum, nonstandardly
20 Sprites are similar to them
22 :, at times
23 "The Ground Beneath ___ Feet" (U2 song)
25 Go a long way
26 Rapper with the 2002 #1 hit "Always on Time"
28 1972 treaty subjects, briefly
31 Like many ventilation systems
35 Dress-to-impress attire
37 Singer Carmen
38 Fukuda's predecessor as Japan's P.M.
39 Italian game akin to pétanque
40 Football Hall-of-Famer who became a Minnesota Supreme Court justice
42 Thirst
43 Genre for 37-Across
44 Ice cream or pizza follower
46 Won't shut up
48 Comment while putting something away
49 Yuri's beloved, in literature
53 More prone to bellyaches
56 Growled at, say
58 Welcomed to one's house
59 One may be represented by stars
61 Plagued
62 Became fair
63 Shakespeare's Ross, e.g.
64 Gift for a TV buff

DOWN

1 Studier of sutras
2 Final aim, to a philosopher
3 Title site of six films: Abbr.
4 He wrote "No human thing is of serious importance"
5 Old story intro?
6 Gull's cry
7 Rip up
8 Strict follower?
9 Stamp feature, in philately lingo
10 Fierce sort
11 What a 64-Across may comprise
12 What a day trader tries to turn
13 Supervillain from Krypton
14 M.D.'s with tiny flashlights
21 Travel plans: Abbr.
24 Like 49-Down
26 Major mode of transportation?
27 Pace of "Pushing Daisies"
29 Many sit on pads
30 Start moving
31 Baroque "key of glory": Abbr.
32 Carol Burnett's 17-Across
33 It's unlikely to work
34 Like Jane Goodall's study site
36 Means of reaching a peak level?
38 "Lord," in Turkish
41 View from a pew
42 Where one may have personal reactions?
45 Put up with
47 Role for both Burton and Amos in a 1977 miniseries
49 Stuff in a swim cap
50 They're not basic things
51 Noël Coward's "Sigh No More," e.g.
52 Ace
53 & 54 Start of a historic telegraph message
55 Invoice abbr.
57 Tutee of Seneca
60 Year in Claudius's reign

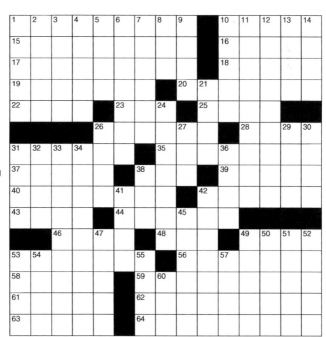

by Julian Lim

60

ACROSS

1 "Another Cinderella Story" co-star, 2008
12 Focus of middle management?
15 Creator of the heroine Catherine Earnshaw
16 It's bisected by the Reuss River
17 City in the 42-Down Desert
18 Caesar's thing
19 N.Y.C. line to the Bronx
20 Race space
21 Name on a London hall
23 Poseidon's trident?
24 Channel with the tagline "Story matters here"
25 10th-century European king
26 First name in gossip
28 Like some issues
32 Like saved hockey shots
35 Gets along
36 English Channel feeder
37 Advice-disdaining sort
40 Mismatched pair?
43 Bearers of bright red arils
44 They're shortsighted
48 See
51 Neighbor of Eure-et-Loir
52 Broadway's "Never ___ Dance"
53 Shogunate capital
56 "Stuff like that"
57 One of reality TV's "Guidettes"
59 Means of enforcing compliance
60 Asian winter celebration
61 Credit card co. concern

62 Two-time Triple Crown winner
65 Operation Cyclone org.
66 Epitome of dedication, in modern usage
67 Either of two cousin Udalls: Abbr.
68 They're suitable to be transplanted to another bed

DOWN

1 Not quite minor-league
2 "The American Scholar" speech giver
3 TV Guide datum
4 She, in Rio
5 Spiral-horned antelope
6 Norm of "This Old House"
7 Mean sort
8 Slow flow
9 6 string
10 View from Biancavilla
11 With fire
12 Golden
13 "Song of the South" villain
14 Raphael's "___ Madonna"
22 It's often a double-decker
27 Swell
29 Elevator of literature?
30 Add (up)
31 Look elated
33 Challenging question
34 1920–24 owner of Metro Pictures
38 What the U.S. joined in Apr. 1917
39 Bath can

40 Where future Web developers develop?
41 Dessert that's out of this world?
42 ___ Desert (area with saguaros)
45 Test-record, maybe
46 Typist, at times
47 Divisions of geometry
49 Game with 59-Down cards
50 Regarding this point
54 Frank account
55 Not estos or esos
58 Pensée product
59 See 49-Down
63 "Hawaii Five-0" co-star Daniel ___ Kim
64 Trig function

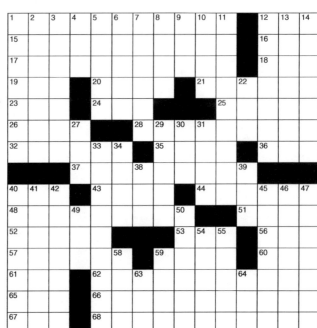

by David Steinberg

ACROSS

1 In-box material for some agents
8 Red, white and blue group
15 Stock pantomime character
16 Decorative server
17 Ahead
18 Wise words
19 Prefix with car
20 Boglike
22 Puts one's foot down
23 A cyclone is a big one
24 Wisconsin port
26 Bad start?
27 Put to work
32 Writer of the lines "Pigeons on the grass alas. / Pigeons on the grass alas"
35 "The Mikado" weapon
36 Emperor who built the Domus Aurea
37 Gerontologist's study
40 You might hear a children's song in one
41 Some fairy story villains
42 Dispatch
43 Watching the big game, say
45 Army missions
46 Like Rome, it's said
48 Blue, in a way: Abbr.
51 Defiant response
55 Skating spot, maybe
56 Symbol of elasticity, in economics
57 Paper work
59 Server of food that may be steamed, fried or raw
61 Went in tandem?
62 Many are found on beaches
63 Gets down
64 Nonsense

DOWN

1 Door-to-door delivery
2 Important part of mayo
3 Plant more crops in
4 N.Y.C. line
5 Alpha senior?
6 One side in the Revolutionary War
7 Serious
8 Common 31-Down: Abbr.
9 Saltier
10 Neither good nor evil
11 Dance element
12 Iris's location
13 Orangish gem
14 Wall St. manipulators
21 1968 #2 hit with the lyric "My love for you is way out of line"
25 Dance elements

26 Mustang competitor
28 Inti worshipers
29 End of a dictionary
30 At one time in the past?
31 Prescribed amount
32 Town in '44 headlines
33 Gracile
34 Ones unable to swim straight?
35 Bag
38 "Kiss Me, Kate" song
39 "Gimme a break!"
44 XX
45 Annie once played by Ethel Merman
47 Iridescent material
48 Messing around on TV?
49 Members of les Nations Unies
50 Reed section?

51 Items in buckets
52 Forte
53 Privateer who captained the Blessed William
54 Quaint shout
58 They may be checked at an airport
60 Part of a barn

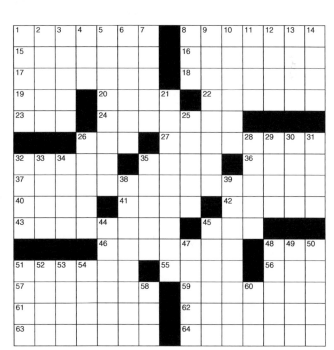

by Gareth Bain

ACROSS

1 What many checks are for
12 Eyebrow-raising
15 One holding the line
16 Man, to Marcus
17 Alternative to lemon chiffon
18 1960s Greystoke portrayer
19 Chelsea-to-Chinatown dir.
20 Like some evidence in arson cases
21 More likely to encounter
23 Label for the Bee Gees
24 Handles
25 Rajiv's mother
28 Victor Herbert's "naughty" girl
29 Thomas called the Queen of Memphis Soul
30 Long meals?
31 Hall monitors, briefly
32 Like Bush Sr., religiously
33 Pod : whales :: knot : ___
34 Land animals?
35 Quick "ha ha"
36 Apt to strike out
37 Sidewalk scam
38 A wide variety
40 Went back and forth
41 Notably high populace
42 Joins
43 He signed 5-Down in 1940
44 Bark part
45 Bitter, e.g.
48 Chemical ending
49 London tabloid
52 Laugh, in Lille
53 1994 Olympic skating champion
54 One of a pair of fraternal twins, maybe
55 Neighbor of the Gem of Gem of the Mountains

DOWN

1 Nicknames
2 Terminal projections, briefly
3 Cabinetry option
4 Motor additive?
5 "Witchcraft" singer
6 Minnesota county west of St. Louis
7 Large lunar crater
8 "Live at the ___" (Patsy Cline album)
9 Biblical boater, in Brest
10 Colombian cowboys
11 Mocha residents
12 Very tense
13 Dabbler
14 Like some nuts
22 Punch choice
23 Has something
24 Having missed the bell, say
25 Their anthem is "Lofsöngur"
26 Son of Marie Louise of Austria
27 Its boring bits can be quite long
28 Liver and kidney
30 Has over
33 Japanese glaze
34 Bikers' mounts
36 Finely tempered swords
37 Game requiring many plug-ins?
39 Nordic flier
40 Home to Liszt and Goethe
42 American Revolution's "Mad Anthony"
44 Pomeranian, e.g.
45 Cantatrice's delivery
46 Yahoo
47 First name in mystery
50 25-Down occupy one: Abbr.
51 Landfill visitor

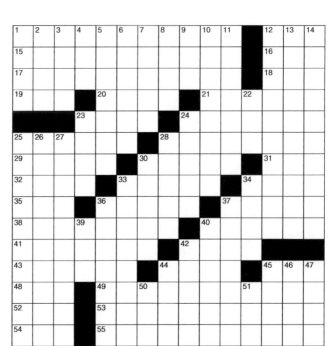

by Michael Wiesenberg

ACROSS

1 "Spin the Black Circle" Grammy winner of 1995
9 Sort who needs to button up
15 Buttoned up
17 Not have a hunch?
18 What shy people often have
19 Trendy tuna
20 With 22-Across, runner's woe
21 Prohibition, e.g.
22 See 20-Across
24 City near Pyramid Lake
25 Uglify
27 "Superman II" villainess
29 Atlas offerings
37 Ivory tower setting
38 Some expressions of false humility
39 Large wire
40 "Boxing Helena" star Sherilyn
41 Squad leader?
42 Comic response, in Variety
45 Greek restaurant menu subheading
48 Realization vocalization
51 Plumber's union?
52 Catcher of the rye?
53 Dipsticks
55 Part of the Ring of Fire
60 Light alternative
61 Modern resident of ancient Ebla
62 Many gallerygoers

DOWN

1 ___-Calais (French department)
2 Imparter of fruity overtones
3 Hub for Jordan Aviation
4 Half-pint
5 Eyeshades?
6 Vingt-et-un, e.g.
7 How some instruments are sold
8 Gessen who wrote the 2012 Putin biography "The Man Without a Face"
9 Bayou predator
10 Cold war grp.?
11 "___ gather"
12 Military brass
13 Horror-struck, apparently
14 First moment
16 Goose
22 Ferry ride, say
23 Ushers in
24 Assault team
25 Depart from
26 Punish by fine
28 They get stuck in corners
29 Arizona's ___ Fria River
30 Some of a caterer's inventory
31 Upscale Italian shoe brand
32 Where Captain Cook landed in 1770
33 "___ first . . ."
34 Conductor Leibowitz
35 Crew at a pileup
36 Short term?
42 Toronto team, briefly
43 Dental gold, e.g.
44 Jacinthe or jonquille
46 Salon service
47 Late notices?
48 Peeved, after "in"
49 Play both sides, in a way
50 Pro grps.
53 Xanadu's river
54 It may have a row of 28-Down, briefly
56 William Tell territory
57 Old Eastern alternative
58 Rankin who created Inspector Rebus
59 Juice fiend

by Martin Ashwood-Smith

64

ACROSS

1 Best-selling Apple app
11 "The Kudlow Report" airer
15 It burns quickly
16 Currency whose name can become its country's name by changing its last letter to an N and scrambling
17 Outlaws
18 Prefix with phobia
19 Like some pliers
20 Fashion inits.
21 O.A.S. member
22 Symbols of innocence
24 Some Southerners
28 Supporter to keep a watchful eye on
30 Cup, maybe
31 Shade of red
32 They're not definite
34 Wistful plaint
35 Lock that's hard to open?
36 Not procrastinating
37 Point of writing
38 ___ Club
39 Rub
40 Naturalist who coined the term "invertebrate"
42 Powerful engine
43 Music style of La Mafia
44 ___-de-Marne (department near Paris)
45 Go up against
46 Children's book ending
53 It may be pasteurisé
54 Complete
55 Colosseum cry
56 Its highest rank is Wonsu
57 Big TV announcement, informally
58 Like Barack Obama's early schoolmates

DOWN

1 "How's it ___ ?"
2 Rice on shelves
3 Bundle of nerves
4 Blasted through
5 Anadem
6 Some council members
7 Comics sound
8 Western gas brand
9 What the picky pick
10 Uncheck, say
11 One may be a rocker
12 Singer with the platinum album "Pink Friday"
13 Five-time Emmy-winning role
14 Sugar sometimes does it
23 Shade of black
24 "Thief" star, 1981
25 Not recently
26 California-based smoothie chain
27 Suffix with press
28 Open
29 "The Battle With the Slum" writer
31 Eastern ___
33 Reinstate, in a way
35 Small meat-stuffed pastries
36 Bit of resistance
38 Certain computer grouping, for short
39 Trattoria selection
41 Ready to be framed, say
42 Banging noise
43 Much lore
44 A clip may come from it
47 Part of the earth's history
48 Reddish-brown quartz
49 H's
50 Adriatic seaport
51 Italian verse form
52 Kirk ___, first actor to play Superman on the big screen

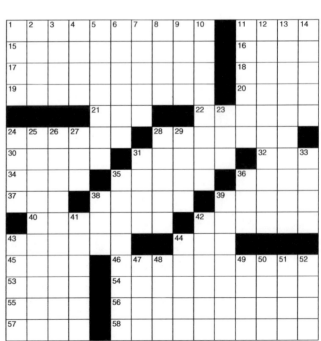

by David Steinberg

ACROSS

1 Stopped living the high life?
10 One paid to get shot
15 Legendary lutist
16 TV host Chung
17 Asia Minor, e.g.
18 Dumps
19 Trail rider's accessory
20 Public
21 Draft pick
22 One highly unlikely to react
24 Geneses
28 Character in "Unforgiven"
29 French verse
30 2011 All-Star pitcher Correia
31 Flow controller
32 He was born "all over like an hairy garment"
33 See 28-Down
34 Trail rider's concoction
35 Gov. Cuomo's purview
36 "Bless ___" (1941 hit song)
37 Slow march, maybe
38 Player in a pocket
40 Holy smoker?
41 Title character singing in the "Tea for Two" duet
42 Not be a wallflower
43 Scrape
44 0–0
50 "Allahu ___" (Iraqi flag phrase)
51 Drill command involving a rifle
52 Whoopi's first leading film role
53 One who doesn't click in a clique
54 Graph revelation, possibly
55 Nonrevolutionaries

DOWN

1 Easy marks
2 Olive genus
3 Ring
4 Old-time actress Bennett
5 Went long
6 Ill-fated line of the 1950s
7 Beefy Provencal stew
8 "The Producers" sex kitten
9 Landscaping alternative to sand
10 Study principally
11 Biblically named Michigan college
12 They don't do it all themselves
13 Monster
14 Common religious artwork
23 "Scratch thee but with ___ . . .": Shak.
24 Bill starter
25 Snoop
26 Like unsurprising temperatures
27 Source of 13-Down eggs
28 With 33-Across, "The Voice" vocal coach
30 Ed whose entire 18-season career was with the Mets
33 Common B-school requirement
34 Spirit in a sling
36 In the log, say
37 Right-handed
39 Hold up
40 Its patrons are usually kept in the dark
42 Blouse with a sailor collar
45 Great Seal word
46 Legal scholar Guinier
47 Symbol of love
48 Sanitization target
49 Former faves of jet-setters

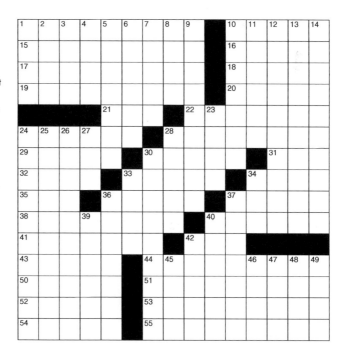

by Chris A. McGlothlin

ACROSS

1 "Good point"
11 Right hand: Abbr.
15 Yarn suppliers?
16 What severe cuts may result in, briefly
17 Lacking in drawing power?
18 Succumb to interrogation
19 Roughly half of all N.B.A. M.V.P.'s
20 Will Rogers props
22 Flavoring compound
23 Resident of Angola, Brazil or Lebanon
25 Ne'er-do-well who stayed out for a long time?
29 Darth, in his boyhood
32 Mulberry cousin
33 It's marked way down
34 Sweet-tempered type
36 Argue
38 Sylvia of jazz
39 For the stated value
41 Something to believe in
43 Getaway destination
44 #5 of the American Film Institute's all-time top 100 movie villains
47 Composer who said "Give me a laundry list and I'll set it to music"
48 U.S. city that's a girl's name
52 Hole
53 Boost
55 "Alias" actress
56 Creator of Wildfell Hall
59 Different
60 Law still in effect but no longer enforced
61 Mr. __ (moniker for Andrei Gromyko)
62 Show with a peanut gallery

DOWN

1 Twinkling
2 Waistband brand
3 "Impossible"
4 Many a laundromat patron
5 Stopgap
6 Move around
7 Angel Clare's wife, in literature
8 Groovy track?
9 Altdorf is its capital
10 What money may be placed in
11 Stigmas
12 Quaint toe clamp tighteners
13 Green light?
14 Sounds of admonishment
21 Cow-horned deity
23 Swiss alternative
24 "Almost there . . ."
26 Super __
27 Planet destroyed in 2009's "Star Trek"
28 Jewelry designer Peretti
29 Chiropractor on "Two and a Half Men"
30 "Of course!"
31 Be a make-up artist?
35 Where a new delivery may be placed?
37 Villain's sinister syllable
40 Ubiquitous prescription
42 Like items on Christmas lists
45 Setting of King Fahd Road
46 Fireflite of the 1950s, e.g.
49 Measures taken slowly?
50 Quiet and soft
51 Impressionism?
52 Either "True Grit" director
53 "Tennessee Waltz" lyricist __ Stewart
54 Without fumbling
57 Con's opening?
58 Hick's nix

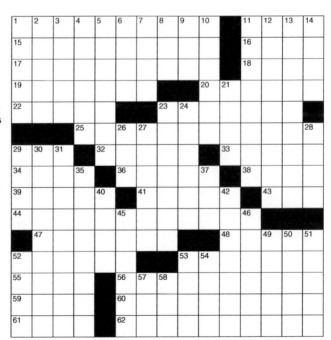

by Doug Peterson and Brad Wilber

ACROSS

1 Chest piece
7 St. John's, for one
15 Fish that attaches itself to a host
16 Like the Congressional Record
17 Biblical prophet whose name means "Yahweh is my God"
18 Act in "The Last Samurai"
19 St. John's, for one
20 Kneecap, e.g.
22 Dick and Al, recently
23 Like King Sargon II: Abbr.
25 33-Down, taking into account its 61-Across
27 Author of "Herding Cats: A Life in Politics"
29 Latin rock band featured at Woodstock
33 Where the guarani is cash
37 Milk source, to a kid
38 Vein gloriousness?
39 Pope who started the First Crusade
41 Tokyo Rose's real first name
42 German chocolate brand
44 Good occasion for kite-flying
46 Shows an aptitude for
48 Mother of the Titans
49 32-Down, taking into account its 61-Across
51 Home of more than 900 volcanoes
55 White House girl
58 Western setting
60 Just under half a penny's weight
61 Place
63 Ostrich, e.g.
65 1950s H-bomb test site
66 Dermatological concern
67 Classic graduation gifts
68 The Missouri, to the Mississippi

DOWN

1 ___ blank
2 Transfers often entail them, informally
3 Bahrain bigwigs: Var.
4 John Paul II, originally
5 Span of a ruler, maybe
6 First name in Chicago politics
7 Part of the coast of Brazil
8 Estée Lauder fragrance for men
9 TV or monitor part: Abbr.
10 "Beats me!"
11 Did with enjoyment
12 Ellington band vocalist Anderson
13 68-Across, taking into account its 61-Across
14 Father/daughter fighters
21 Take ___ at
24 Iran, North Korea and the like
26 Veneer, e.g.
28 Ask, as for assistance
30 It's not basic
31 Astronomical figure?
32 Out
33 Strong wine
34 "La donna è mobile," e.g.
35 Give off, with "of"
36 Not pitch or roll, say
40 Big uranium exporter
43 Twin-engine Navy helicopter
45 Site of the Three Gorges Dam
47 Hoofing it
50 Abruptly stops, with "out"
52 Like mummies
53 Instruction written in currants for Alice
54 Campaign dirty trick
55 Coast, in a way
56 1-Across, taking into account its 61-Across
57 Univ. grouping
59 Nonkosher
62 Samson's end?
64 Pal

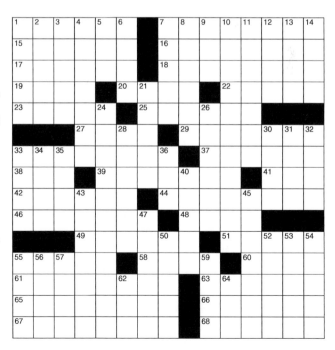

by Matt Ginsberg

ACROSS

1 What you may charge with
16 Indicator of how accurate a numerical guess is
17 Bringer of peace
18 The look of love?
19 One built for Broadway
20 Intel processor?
21 Pliers part
24 "The Chronicles of Clovis" author
26 Running dog
32 Opposite of extremely
34 Curing stuff, symbolically
36 Heffalump's creator
37 Title gambler in a 1943 Cary Grant film
39 Northern game preceder
41 Waits awhile
42 Eagles tight end Igwenagu
44 Make canning impossible?
45 Much commercial production
47 Flat
49 Some holiday honorees: Abbr.
50 Start of a Vol. 1 heading
52 Post-W.W. II fed. agcy.
54 Tone poem that calls for four taxi horns, with "An"
63 Past pump preference
64 Packing it in
65 Information information

DOWN

1 Some of them have learned to sign
2 Blowout locale?
3 "Thou ___ lady": King Lear
4 They might design roses
5 Visual aids
6 Like bazookas
7 1930s bomber
8 Not windy at all
9 Painter Schiele and composer Wellesz
10 Life is one
11 Their caps have a stylized "C"
12 Language related to Wyandot
13 Transporter of beer barrels
14 Captive of Heracles
15 Quarter of doce
21 Window parts
22 Like some anchors and sails
23 Not just another face in the crowd?
25 "The Inspector General" star, 1949
27 Org. that publishes Advocacy Update
28 Quarter of vingt
29 "Revolver" Grammy winner Voormann
30 Split up
31 "Deirdre" playwright
33 Certain recital piece
35 Kind of chop
38 Chi setting
40 One of several Procter & Gamble products
43 Chandra, in Hindu belief
46 Like a lot without a lot
48 Boot
51 Porsche 911 model
53 ___-foot jelly
54 Many masters respond to them
55 Cross
56 Hohenberg's river
57 Like line jumpers
58 First name in '70s tennis
59 Martin Buber's "___ Thou"
60 Shore indentations
61 Thomas H. ___, the Father of the Western
62 Calls on

by Martin Ashwood-Smith

ACROSS

1 What's "all in my brain," in a 1967 rock classic
11 Dynasty founded by Yu the Great
15 Like some majors and wars
16 Capping
17 Be peerless
18 Blacks out
19 Little Joe's half brother of old TV
20 Einstein's death
21 Preakness, e.g.
22 Image mentale
24 First created being, in myth
26 Stand-up comic known for irreverent sermonettes
31 Form's top, perhaps
32 Make inseparable
33 River forming the Handegg waterfall
34 Having one 49-Across
35 Winner of seven tennis majors in the 1920s
38 Material in the translation process
39 Caterpillar roll ingredient
40 Operation creation
41 Java class?
43 Do a vanishing act
47 Jezebel's lack
48 One housed in a chest
49 See 34-Across
51 "Dear" one
52 Diamond stats
56 Decimal starter
57 Microsoft Office feature
60 Figure taking a bow?
61 No-strings declaration?
62 ___ deal
63 "So Wrong" singer, 1962

DOWN

1 Labor leader's cry?
2 It may precede itself
3 Stds. for A and E, e.g.
4 Seriously thinking
5 Monitor option, briefly
6 High
7 Headbands?
8 Longtime teammate of Mr. November
9 Eastern state?
10 City near Utrecht
11 Violent sandstorm
12 Old TV show hosted by Ed McMahon
13 Makeup of some beams
14 Basilica niche
21 Submitted
23 Product named for its "'round the clock protection"

24 Broccoli bits?
25 Foil component
26 Building with many sides
27 Fifth-century invader
28 ___-one
29 Stormed
30 Winner of 14 tennis majors in the 1990s
31 Wasn't straight
36 Many a college interviewer
37 Reference
42 Cylindrical menu item
44 What outer space is that cyberspace isn't?
45 Circular stack
46 Epsom's setting
49 Leave one's coat behind?
50 Saving type
51 Performer of high-risk operations

53 Mideastern P.M.'s nickname
54 Not blind to
55 Affliction whose name rhymes with its location
57 Vegas spot
58 German granny
59 American Crossroads, e.g.

by David Steinberg

ACROSS

1 Stephen King horror anthology
10 Yoke attachment
15 Great depression?
16 Egg choice
17 They're available in alleys
18 Wholly
19 Short play?
20 The King's followers?
21 Like some taxes and questions
22 Considered revolting
24 Struck
25 Pick
26 Home of the Aggies of the 37-Down
31 Below the surface
34 Québec map abbr.
35 Arena support?
36 Remove, as a 45-Across
38 Grand alternative
41 Trip option: Abbr.
42 She plagues ladies' lips with blisters, per Mercutio
44 Game of falling popularity?
45 It fits around a mouth
49 Bangladesh export
50 Using
51 Aviation safety statistic
55 What's often blowing in the wind
58 Show piece
59 Floral arrangement
60 Floor plan data
61 Painful spa treatment
63 Had an inclination
64 Nevertheless
65 Roman world
66 Justice from the Bronx

DOWN

1 What a speaker may strike
2 Nepalese bread
3 Classic Meccano toy
4 Midwest trailer?
5 Embedded column
6 Hardly any
7 Haydn's "master of us all"
8 Upstate New York natives
9 Unseld of the Bullets
10 Twist in fiction
11 Hit soundtrack album of 1980
12 Stationery securer
13 Look while delivering a line
14 Metalworker's union?
21 Leaving out
23 Grand
27 Good name for a brooder?
28 How many reach the top of Pikes Peak
29 Not grade-specific
30 Loses liquidity
31 Bellflower or Bell Gardens, vis-à-vis L.A.
32 Quaint preposition
33 Put down
37 New Mexico State sports grp.
39 "Cloth diaper" or "film camera"
40 Bullet follower
43 Frito ___ (old ad symbol)
46 Cable channel with the slogan "Laugh More"
47 Doesn't level with
48 Check out for a second
52 Certain building block, informally
53 Former defense grp.
54 Knick foe
55 One with hot dates, maybe
56 ___ Biscuit (1912 debut)
57 Spare
61 Low, in Lyon
62 Portfolio part, for short

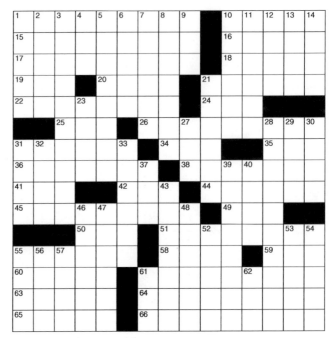

by Barry C. Silk

ACROSS

1 One was first purchased in 2008
10 Big top features?
15 Title for Schwarzenegger
16 Half of a TV duo
17 One going through the exercises?
18 Leader of the Silver Bullet Band
19 Silence fillers
20 One might be apparent
21 See
22 Bit
24 "Toast of the Town" host
28 Grunt
29 1991 International Tennis Hall of Fame inductee
30 Cliff dweller
31 Ambulance supply
34 Game with points
35 Tired
36 Outfielder who was a member of baseball's All-Century Team
40 Digs, with "on"
42 ___ glass
43 1955 doo-wop hit
46 Peace Nobelist Cassin
47 Crooked bones?
51 Trix alternative?
52 Construction support
53 Drying device
55 2012 Seth MacFarlane comedy
56 Sound
58 Oath
60 Impala relative
61 Crisp salad ingredient from across the Pacific
62 Satisfy
63 Child support payer, in modern lingo

DOWN

1 "Can't wait!"
2 Opening
3 Item used in an exotic massage
4 Cheer with an accent
5 When doubled, a taunt
6 Host
7 Horticultural headache
8 Some landings
9 6 is a rare one
10 From overseas?
11 Lending figure
12 Northern Quebec's ___ Peninsula
13 Some Vatican art
14 Still
23 Athlete's booster
25 Ally
26 Race assignments
27 W.W. II inits.
31 Rose

32 Full of oneself
33 Roman numeral that's also a name
37 Like most sandals
38 Moneymaker topping a Web site
39 Milk and milk and milk
41 Common cocktail component
43 Common cocktail components
44 Cricket violation
45 Yellow Teletubby
48 2008 documentary about the national debt
49 Antilles native
50 Bacon product
54 Mind
57 W.W. II inits.
58 Meter site
59 New Deal program, for short

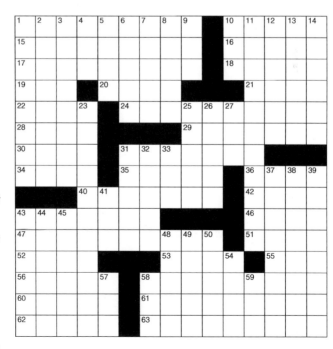

by David Quarfoot

ACROSS

1 Place to pick vegetables
9 With 25-Across, it has a huge trunk
15 C-worthy
16 Ancient abstainer
17 Buzzer sounded during a match
18 Small house of the Southwest
19 Whence Parmenides
20 Bubkes
22 See 23-Across
23 With 22-Across, quits dragging
25 See 9-Across
27 Special recognition?
28 They result when solidly hit baseballs are caught
31 Royale maker
32 Major cleanups follow them
35 Starting catcher in every All-Star Game from 1964 to 1967
37 Name meaning "God is with us"
38 Go
40 Four French quarters?
41 They're likely to result in broken limbs
43 Claptrap
44 Prey for gray wolves
46 It has a Bridges and Tunnels div.
47 "Home away from home" sloganeer
48 "Until next time"
52 Vindictive Quaker of fiction
54 Like unabridged dictionaries
57 Angel, e.g., for short
58 Wonder Lake's national park
60 It stays the same
62 Site of a 1944 British Army defeat
63 Nourishing stuff
64 Treating badly
65 "S.N.L." segment

DOWN

1 Takes into account?
2 No longer in the minority
3 Bad thing to be breached
4 Water board
5 Old brand that promised "white white washes without red hands"
6 Guthrie's follower at Woodstock
7 Hun king, in myth
8 Frequent tour guide
9 Saxophone great Sidney
10 White sheet insert?
11 Fêmur, por exemplo
12 Goof
13 Herpetologist's supply
14 Six Gallery reading participants
21 Like some garlic and egos
24 "I goofed . . . big whoop"
26 Heir restoration targets?
29 Gas hog, briefly
30 Lock remover of old?
32 Formal opening
33 Answering machine notification
34 1836 siege leader
36 Sole mate?
39 Journal ender
42 Some Toyotas
45 Last month
49 Ethiopian grazer
50 Gossip girl
51 Like craft fairs
53 German way
55 Buzz on "The Simpsons," e.g.
56 Use a ball winder
59 Cry from some judges
61 Conference USA member, for short

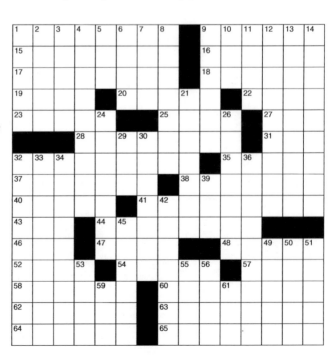

by Ned White

ACROSS

1. Old easy-to-load shooter
11. Comparative follower
15. Pitching technique?
16. Government auction action
17. Toe-tapping trigger
18. Kissers
19. Some fridges
20. Dot in an atlas
21. How close-up magicians move
23. Home of some frogs
24. Fixed a broken web link?
25. Says "You said it!," say
28. Miss swinging at a piñata?
30. Thugs
31. Tiny bit
32. Taste test
33. Memo heads-up
34. Customer counter, maybe
35. Coloring
36. It airs episodes of "Episodes," briefly
37. François's following?
38. Keep the squeaking out of, say
39. It's drawn between similar things
41. Bantam
42. Teaching model
43. Small doses?
44. Green traffic sight?
45. Lift in greeting
46. City and state follower
49. Nero's position?
50. "A Tale of Two Cities" ender?
53. Some Fr. honorees
54. Where the Garden State Parkway meets I-280
55. Lake ___ (largest lake in Australia)
56. Stop on the way from 0 to 60?

DOWN

1. "Cool, bro"
2. Norton Sound port
3. Concessions
4. Skipping sound?
5. Outfits
6. Nephew of Matty and Jesus
7. She released "21" in 2011
8. It might be harsh or hushed
9. It oversees a major production every two yrs.
10. Plausibility
11. Strive to reach
12. One of Superman's powers
13. Cosmo alternatives
14. Busy
22. Battle of Endor combatant
23. Andrew Johnson's home: Abbr.
24. Rocks from socks
25. Audibly amazed
26. Penguin's habitat?
27. Line opener
28. Series of selling points
29. With relevance
31. Winter malady
34. Acts as if money were no object
35. Little props
37. Seltzer starter
38. He starred as Gatsby in 1974
40. Pin something on
41. Cookware cover
43. Very, to Verdi
44. Ovidian infinitive
45. Either side of an Oreo
46. Fan's pub
47. Young Frankenstein married her
48. Kind of review
51. Fujairah's locale: Abbr.
52. Hanger in a clothing shop

by Bruce Sutphin and Doug Peterson

ACROSS

1 Bloke
5 Proper partner?
9 Expressed out loud
11 Big name in folk music
13 Cubs cap display
15 Patroness of Québec
16 Defeat in a jump-rope competition, say
17 It's said to be the world's fastest field sport
18 More in need of a bath, say
19 Craigslist and others
20 Make sense
22 Rocker with the 1973 #1 hit "Frankenstein"
23 Spotted horse
24 Helpers for the deaf
30 Loitering
32 Arrangement of atoms in a crystal structure
33 Accounting department employees
35 Muscle that rotates a part outward
36 Definitely not a good looker?
37 "Standing room only"
38 Wash
39 Some jazz combos
40 Join up for another collaboration
41 Middling
42 Georgia and neighbors, once: Abbr.

DOWN

1 French hearts
2 Member of an ancient people known for warfare with chariots
3 Pretends to be sore
4 Christmas no-no
5 Views through a periscope, say
6 "It is through Art, and through Art only, that we can ___ our perfection": Oscar Wilde
7 Furnace part
8 Speed Stick brand
9 Certain YouTube posting
10 Little orange snacks
11 Sign over a car
12 Rules and ___
14 Some E.M.T. personnel
15 Living like husband and wife
21 Unpaid
24 Really would rather not
25 Menu heading
26 Hurriedly, in scores
27 Sedimentary rocks resembling cemented fish roe
28 Throats
29 Elvis Presley, notably
30 Post-hurricane scenes, e.g.
31 Fuel line additive
32 One side of a famous NBC feud
34 Look

by Joe Krozel

ACROSS

1 "Moses" novelist
5 Home to Morro Castle
9 Rigging pros
14 Hoops nickname
15 Its prices are determined by competition
17 Rafts
18 "Red pottage" in Genesis
19 Gun
20 Sharks' place
21 Neighbor of Telescopium
22 "___ Obama" (epithet used by Rush Limbaugh)
24 Criticize in a small way, informally
25 Circulation problem
26 "Just ___ Love Her" (1950 hit)
28 Granny, to Gretel
30 Central figure of a country
38 1978 punk classic
39 Transcript, e.g.
40 What many married couples bring in
41 Finnair alternative
42 Blowout, e.g.
43 With 5-Down, bygone beverage
46 Sort who isn't safe around a safe
50 "Women Ironing" artist
53 English Channel feeder
54 I and above, to Sonorans
56 Honor for Harry Potter's creator: Abbr.
57 Acid Queen player in "Tommy"
59 1998 Spielberg title role
60 "Two Tickets to Paradise" singer

61 Domino getting played
62 They take up some measures
63 Squat
64 Gonitis target

DOWN

1 1960s TV dog
2 Walk-ins?
3 It may cover all the bases
4 C.E.O.'s places
5 See 43-Across
6 Knock for a loop
7 Dog star
8 Composer Arensky
9 Roll in the grass?
10 Sites for system repairs, briefly
11 Toasting option
12 Intro to chemistry?
13 Parade honoree, familiarly

16 What a bad ruler does
20 Parting word
23 Mizzen neighbor
25 Dressage half-turn
27 Put away, maybe
29 1970s
30 Sots' shots
31 ___ bit
32 Look out for, say
33 Singer Lovich
34 Sparkling white
35 "Chloe" director, 2009
36 "Chicago" Golden Globe winner
37 Teaching degs.
43 2012 major-league leader in hits
44 Quicklime, e.g.
45 Furnishes
47 ___ Field (Minute Maid Park, once)

48 Fixin' to
49 "Wall Street" theme
51 Drop off
52 What a yo-yo lacks
54 Tour de France times
55 Sam Cooke's "___ Little Love"
58 British isle
59 Subj. of the 2006 film "Bobby"

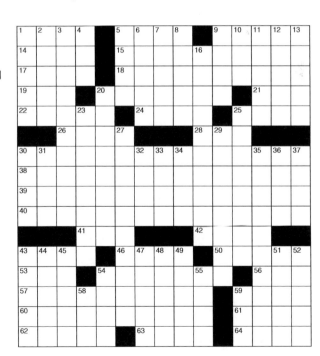

by Martin Ashwood-Smith

The New York Times

SMART PUZZLES
Presented with Style

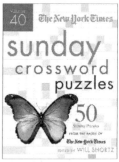

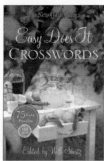
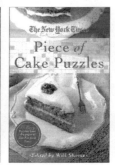

1

S	Q	U	A	B	B	L	E	■	J	A	M	C	A	M
E	U	P	H	O	R	I	A	■	O	R	I	O	L	E
T	I	P	S	H	E	E	T	■	K	I	D	U	L	T
B	B	S	■	M	A	L	I	C	E	■	E	L	S	E
A	B	A	S	■	K	O	T	O	■	H	A	D	T	O
I	L	L	I	N	■	W	U	N	D	E	R	B	A	R
L	E	A	N	O	N	■	P	I	E	R	■	E	R	S
■	■	S	O	U	P	■	C	L	O	P	■	■	■	■
S	E	A	■	G	T	O	S	■	L	I	T	O	U	T
E	X	Q	U	I	S	I	T	E	■	C	A	N	S	O
A	T	U	N	E	■	S	U	C	H	■	S	E	T	T
G	R	I	P	■	D	E	C	A	Y	S	■	M	I	A
R	E	V	I	S	E	■	K	R	A	T	I	O	N	S
A	M	E	L	I	E	■	U	T	T	E	R	R	O	T
M	E	R	E	S	T	■	P	E	T	P	E	E	V	E

2

B	U	T	T	D	I	A	L	E	D	■	G	I	B	E
O	N	A	R	A	M	P	A	G	E	■	U	N	O	S
T	I	D	A	L	B	A	S	I	N	■	M	O	B	S
S	T	A	P	L	E	R	■	S	A	C	■	N	S	A
■	■	P	A	C	T	S	■	L	O	V	E	L	Y	■
I	C	E	■	S	I	M	I	■	I	N	A	P	E	T
N	A	N	S	■	L	E	T	S	■	A	S	I	D	E
B	R	I	E	F	E	N	C	O	U	N	T	E	R	S
A	D	D	E	R	■	T	O	R	N	■	S	C	U	T
D	E	B	T	E	E	■	M	E	I	N	■	E	N	S
S	A	L	O	O	N	■	S	L	O	O	P	■	■	■
O	L	Y	■	N	A	M	■	O	N	S	E	R	V	E
R	E	T	D	■	C	A	S	S	I	O	P	E	I	A
T	R	O	Y	■	T	A	K	E	S	A	S	E	A	T
S	S	N	S	■	S	M	A	R	T	P	I	L	L	S

3

A	P	P	L	E	C	A	R	E	■	R	A	N	C	H
D	O	U	B	L	E	B	E	D	■	O	M	A	H	A
I	M	T	O	O	S	E	X	Y	■	M	A	T	E	Y
D	E	T	■	N	A	Y	A	■	O	A	T	E	R	S
A	L	E	R	■	R	A	L	P	H	■	D	O	E	■
S	O	R	O	S	■	N	L	R	B	■	P	O	K	E
■	■	S	T	E	T	■	S	A	V	A	G	E	D	■
Z	E	A	L	O	T	■	■	B	I	N	G	E	S	■
A	L	E	Y	A	R	D	■	T	Y	N	E	■	■	■
P	E	O	N	■	A	E	R	O	■	G	R	I	E	G
C	O	N	■	D	R	E	W	U	■	A	N	N	A	■
O	N	F	I	R	E	■	L	A	N	D	■	T	R	I
M	O	L	D	Y	■	F	O	R	C	E	Q	U	I	T
I	R	U	L	E	■	B	A	D	A	D	V	I	C	E
X	A	X	E	S	■	I	N	S	P	E	C	T	O	R

4

J	U	J	I	T	S	U	■	J	A	Z	Z	A	G	E
E	L	A	T	I	O	N	■	S	H	O	O	T	U	P
T	A	K	E	A	I	M	■	B	O	O	T	E	E	S
S	L	A	M	S	■	A	L	A	R	M	■	D	S	T
F	U	R	S	■	S	P	I	C	A	■	V	I	S	E
A	M	T	■	D	E	P	T	H	■	F	A	R	S	I
N	E	A	T	I	D	E	A	■	S	A	L	T	O	N
■	■	A	C	E	D	■	■	Z	A	N	E	■	■	■
F	I	B	B	E	R	■	H	A	N	G	T	I	M	E
A	P	L	U	S	■	P	A	N	T	S	■	C	O	X
S	A	I	S	■	L	A	N	Z	A	■	B	A	R	T
T	N	T	■	A	U	S	S	I	■	P	E	N	T	E
C	E	Z	A	N	N	E	■	B	U	I	L	T	I	N
A	M	E	R	I	G	O	■	A	T	A	C	O	S	T
R	A	N	K	L	E	S	■	R	E	S	H	O	E	S

5

S	G	T	S	C	H	U	L	T	Z	■	C	R	A	B
U	R	A	N	I	U	M	O	R	E	■	L	I	L	O
D	A	T	I	N	G	P	O	O	L	■	U	G	L	Y
S	P	I	T	E	■	I	K	I	D	■	S	H	O	W
Y	E	N	S	■	O	R	S	■	A	C	T	T	W	O
■	■	■	P	A	E	A	N	■	H	E	M	A	N	■
B	I	O	G	A	S	■	T	A	M	A	R	I	N	D
U	N	M	A	T	E	D	■	S	I	L	E	N	C	E
S	T	E	V	E	S	A	X	■	R	E	D	D	E	R
H	E	L	E	N	■	M	R	M	E	T	■	■	■	■
W	R	E	A	T	H	■	A	I	D	■	S	E	T	I
H	A	T	H	■	A	P	T	S	■	P	I	C	O	T
A	L	P	O	■	N	A	I	L	S	A	L	O	N	S
C	I	A	O	■	S	A	N	A	N	T	O	N	I	O
K	A	N	T	■	A	R	G	Y	L	E	S	O	C	K

6

P	R	O	A	C	T	I	V	■	■	B	B	G	U	N
H	A	S	N	O	I	D	E	A	■	P	U	L	S	E
E	M	M	A	S	T	O	N	E	■	O	G	E	E	S
L	E	O	I	■	O	L	D	G	E	E	Z	E	R	■
P	A	N	S	Y	■	O	I	L	■	A	C	N	E	■
S	U	D	■	E	V	E	R	S	O	■	P	L	A	T
■	■	E	T	A	T	S	■	■	P	U	M	A	■	■
O	B	T	A	I	N	S	■	J	E	Z	E	B	E	L
B	A	A	S	■	■	A	I	R	E	R	■	■	■	■
I	C	K	Y	■	D	I	S	B	A	R	■	S	T	U
S	K	E	G	■	O	A	F	■	■	O	C	E	A	N
■	B	O	O	K	S	M	A	R	T	■	H	E	R	D
M	O	V	I	E	■	■	B	R	E	A	K	I	N	T	O
O	N	E	N	D	■	S	A	N	D	A	L	T	A	N
B	E	R	G	S	■	■	S	T	A	L	L	O	N	E

7

■	P	A	N	A	M	G	A	M	E	S	■	P	C	S
D	E	T	E	R	I	O	R	A	T	E	■	H	A	L
T	E	R	R	E	N	C	E	M	C	N	A	L	L	Y
E	T	A	T	S	■	O	T	I	S	■	L	O	V	E
N	E	S	S	■	S	M	E	E	■	F	I	X	E	R
■	■	■	J	A	M	■	■	V	I	P	■	■	■	■
A	N	C	H	O	R	A	G	E	A	L	A	S	K	A
F	O	R	E	I	G	N	M	I	N	I	S	T	E	R
T	R	A	I	N	E	D	E	L	E	P	H	A	N	T
A	N	T	S	I	N	O	N	E	S	P	A	N	T	S
■	T	N	T	■	■	E	S	O	■	■	■	■	■
G	O	B	I	G	■	C	A	N	A	■	A	M	A	T
U	P	O	N	■	W	O	R	F	■	S	C	A	R	E
S	E	R	G	E	A	N	T	O	R	O	U	R	K	E
T	R	A	■	R	I	G	O	R	M	O	R	T	I	S
S	A	X	■	B	L	O	O	D	S	T	A	I	N	■

8

A	N	G	I	E	■	■	N	E	W	Y	O	R	K
P	E	R	K	S	■	S	O	L	E	M	N	E	R
S	H	E	E	T	■	F	U	N	G	I	C	I	D	E
E	R	E	■	T	A	M	P	A	■	A	C	O	W
S	U	N	D	A	Y	W	O	R	L	D	■	E	S	E
■	L	U	M	E	N	■	O	L	E	S	■	■
O	M	A	N	I	S	■	■	O	W	N	E	R	S
R	A	N	D	D	■	■	C	O	S	T	A
O	R	D	E	A	L	■	C	L	O	S	E	D
■	E	L	O	I	■	S	T	A	T	E	■
B	B	S	■	A	R	T	H	U	R	W	Y	N	N	E
E	L	A	M	■	E	W	E	L	L	■	T	E	X
D	A	L	A	I	L	A	M	A	■	C	H	I	R	P
I	N	E	X	C	E	S	S	■	G	U	A	V	A
M	C	M	X	I	I	I	■	I	N	L	E	T

9

J	U	M	B	O	F	R	I	E	S	■	S	R	T	A
O	N	I	O	N	R	I	N	G	S	■	U	I	E	S
G	U	N	S	L	I	N	G	E	R	■	G	P	A	S
S	M	A	■	E	D	G	E	R	■	P	A	S	S	E
■	■	P	A	G	O	■	■	G	A	R	N	E	T
M	O	J	A	V	E	■	S	T	U	C	C	O	■
E	D	U	C	E	■	B	O	R	N	T	O	R	U	N
W	I	S	E	■	B	A	R	A	K	■	A	T	N	O
L	E	T	S	P	A	R	T	Y	■	S	T	E	P	S
■	P	E	O	R	I	A	■	P	I	E	R	C	E
O	D	E	T	T	E	■	M	I	L	D	■	■
F	I	A	T	S	■	A	T	O	L	L	■	D	A	D
O	N	C	E	■	S	M	I	L	E	Y	F	A	C	E
L	A	H	R	■	S	E	N	T	I	M	E	N	T	S
D	R	Y	S	■	A	N	Y	O	N	E	E	L	S	E

10

A	S	I	A	N	■	■	D	J	P	A	U	L	Y	D
C	O	N	D	O	■	G	R	E	A	T	B	E	A	R
T	U	T	O	R	■	L	A	T	C	H	O	N	T	O
U	S	E	R	■	M	I	N	S	K	■	A	D	E	N
P	A	R	K	R	A	N	G	E	R	■	T	A	S	E
■	V	A	U	L	T	■	T	A	B	■	■
C	R	A	B	B	I	E	R	■	T	I	P	P	L	E
P	O	L	L	O	■	D	O	S	■	G	R	A	I	N
R	O	S	E	U	P	■	T	E	E	T	E	R	E	D
■	■	T	A	C	■	A	L	O	F	T	■
A	R	C	S	■	T	H	E	C	A	P	I	T	O	L
M	O	O	T	■	D	I	X	O	N	■	G	I	V	E
A	U	D	I	T	O	R	I	A	■	L	U	M	E	N
S	T	O	N	E	W	A	L	L	■	A	R	E	N	T
S	E	N	T	E	N	C	E	■	V	E	R	S	O

11

```
C A N A D A B L U E G R A S S
T R A D I T I O N A L I R A S
N A V A L E N G A G E M E N T
S T E M L E S S G L A S S E S
█ L A Y █ █ H I E S █ █ █
C D R █ █ S K I █ S O S P A D
R A I D █ R A P S █ N E A L E
I N N O W A Y █ I T S A L O T
S I G M A █ O R Z O █ R E N O
P O S S U M █ O E R █ S E X █
█ █ █ K E R T █ S A T █ █ █
O B S C E N E G E S T U R E S
P O T A S S I U M I O D I D E
E L E P H A N T T R A I N E R
D E N T A L A S S I S T A N T
```

12

```
B A N A N A G R A M S █ U S M
A D O B E R E A D E R █ G E E
T I J U A N A T A X I █ G A G
E D I T █ E R A █ S A B R A
S A V █ C L U T C H █ S O O N
█ S E T H █ P A L O █ P O U F
█ █ A E C █ T E R Z E T T O
I L O V E L A █ F A I R S E X
F A C E P A L M █ E N S █
I V A R █ R E U P █ G E E Z
D A R N █ A C R O S S █ R A G
I T I S I █ █ D I P █ W A N E
D O N █ T A X O N O M I S T S
I R A █ E J E C T O R S E A T
T Y S █ S A S H A F I E R C E
```

13

```
Z O M B I E █ █ S W A M P E D
A N O M A L Y █ S O S U E M E
G E T I N T O █ W R I T E I N
A T O █ S O D A █ D A I N T Y
T O R A █ N E W T O N S █ █
R O C C O █ L O A F █ M S G S
A M Y T A N █ L P G A █ U L U
T A C I T U S █ S O B E R U P
E N L █ S M O G █ D E L E T E
D Y E S █ B O O B █ S H E E R
█ █ T E S T B A N █ I N N S
U N L O C K █ S N E E █ O F T
R A I N O U T █ D R L A U R A
N U T E L L A █ S T I N G E R
S T E R I L E █ S A S H E S
```

14

```
B A R B A R A B U S H █ B E E
E Q U I V A L E N C E █ R R R
F A S C I N A T I O N █ O I L
O B E S █ D R A F T █ W A K E
G A S █ M O M M Y █ L E D S █
█ █ M A M B A █ M A D C A P
A H E A D █ E X F O L I A T E
C A R R O L L █ L E A D S I N
E M I L N O L D E █ K I T E S
D O C E N T █ E X M E T █ █
█ M A N A █ F S T A R █ M E W
Z E K E █ K L E I N █ P I S A
A L A █ Y O U R M A J E S T Y
G E N █ O L I V E G A R D E N
S T E █ U N D E R E X P O S E
```

15

```
B A S █ F L I P O N E S L I D
A C H █ J U K E B O X H E R O
T R A █ O R E G O N T R A I L
H O M B R E █ W I E █ I S N T
S P E E D █ D O S █ Y M H A █
H O L E █ P H O T O O P █ █
E L E C █ O L D S A W █ H E R
B I S H O P █ █ S L E A Z Y
A S S █ D O G S I T █ M I R A
█ █ █ R E V O L T S █ B R A N
█ C B E R █ K O S █ T E M P O
P A R I █ L A V █ H E R E O N
O R A N G E P E K O E █ T U E
S O V I E T U N I O N █ A N A
T B O N E S T E A K S █ L D L
```

16

K	A	M	A	S	U	T	R	A	■	L	O	N	G	S
E	G	O	M	A	N	I	A	C	■	E	N	E	R	O
P	E	N	N	Y	A	N	T	E	■	L	E	G	A	L
T	R	O	I	S	■	T	E	R	R	A	N	O	V	A
■	■	■	O	A	S	■	■	E	N	O	T	E	S	■
S	W	M	■	H	O	U	S	E	M	D	■	I	S	T
T	H	I	S	■	U	S	E	R	S	■	K	A	T	Y
B	A	L	L	■	P	A	X	I	L	■	O	T	O	E
O	L	I	O	■	N	I	E	C	E	■	P	E	N	A
N	E	T	■	M	A	R	S	H	E	S	■	D	E	R
I	B	A	N	E	Z	■	■	■	P	O	M	■	■	■
F	O	R	E	L	I	M	B	S	■	N	A	R	C	S
A	N	I	L	L	■	R	A	T	I	O	N	O	U	T
C	E	E	L	O	■	A	L	A	N	M	O	O	R	E
E	S	S	E	N	■	Z	E	N	G	A	R	D	E	N

17

A	L	C	H	E	M	I	S	T	S	■	B	A	S	E
P	I	R	A	T	E	S	H	I	P	■	O	M	A	R
S	T	A	Y	A	T	H	O	M	E	■	S	E	M	I
E	R	N	S	■	H	O	W	■	D	V	O	R	A	K
S	E	E	T	O	■	T	D	S	■	E	M	I	R	S
■	■	■	A	A	A	■	O	L	A	Y	■	C	I	A
B	L	A	C	K	M	A	G	I	C	■	W	A	T	T
R	I	S	K	S	I	T	■	M	T	S	I	N	A	I
O	P	T	S	■	C	O	M	E	U	N	D	O	N	E
A	R	R	■	J	I	M	I	■	P	E	E	■	■	■
D	E	O	R	O	■	S	N	L	■	E	R	A	S	E
B	A	D	E	G	G	■	I	A	N	■	I	R	A	S
A	D	O	S	■	A	R	C	H	A	N	G	E	L	S
N	E	M	O	■	W	H	A	T	A	S	H	A	M	E
D	R	E	W	■	D	O	M	I	N	A	T	R	I	X

18

L	A	B	A	M	B	A	■	A	T	A	V	I	S	T
I	P	A	D	A	I	R	■	S	I	S	E	N	O	R
R	E	T	W	E	E	T	■	K	T	H	X	B	Y	E
A	S	E	A	■	N	E	B	U	L	A	■	■	■	■
■	■	■	R	E	V	■	O	P	E	N	T	O	P	■
S	U	P	E	R	E	G	O	■	■	T	A	B	L	E
N	N	E	■	S	N	A	K	E	B	I	T	T	E	N
A	C	R	E	■	U	N	C	L	E	■	S	A	D	D
G	O	O	G	L	E	G	L	A	S	S	■	I	T	O
S	I	N	G	E	■	■	U	N	T	I	L	N	O	W
■	L	I	O	N	C	U	B	■	D	R	E	■	■	■
■	■	■	S	E	N	S	O	R	■	F	O	W	L	■
P	A	J	A	M	A	S	■	P	A	D	T	H	A	I
D	V	D	C	A	S	E	■	T	M	O	B	I	L	E
F	I	S	H	N	E	T	■	S	A	M	E	O	L	D

19

J	A	I	L	B	R	E	A	K	■	M	E	C	C	A
A	P	O	L	L	O	X	I	I	■	S	T	O	L	I
C	A	N	D	Y	S	H	O	P	■	D	A	K	A	R
O	T	I	S	■	S	A	L	■	A	O	L	E	R	S
B	O	Z	■	B	I	L	I	O	U	S	■	Z	I	P
S	W	E	A	R	■	E	S	P	N	■	M	E	T	A
■	■	■	T	I	C	S	■	S	T	E	A	R	I	C
M	O	J	I	T	O	■	■	I	N	T	O	N	E	■
O	P	U	L	E	N	T	■	B	E	E	T	■	■	■
N	E	S	T	■	D	R	E	I	■	M	E	S	A	S
A	N	T	■	G	O	I	N	G	B	Y	■	E	R	E
R	A	D	N	E	R	■	C	H	A	■	L	A	I	T
C	R	O	O	N	■	G	O	O	G	L	E	B	O	T
H	E	I	S	T	■	A	R	A	G	O	N	E	S	E
Y	A	T	E	S	■	S	E	X	Y	S	A	D	I	E

20

H	O	L	M	E	S	I	A	N	■	T	B	A	R	S
A	T	A	G	L	A	N	C	E	■	A	R	P	E	L
K	I	S	S	Y	F	A	C	E	■	M	A	P	L	E
E	S	T	■	S	E	N	T	■	H	A	I	L	E	D
■	■	■	T	I	L	E	■	H	O	R	N	E	T	S
S	U	B	W	A	Y	■	S	E	R	I	F	S	■	■
A	L	A	I	N	■	H	U	M	A	N	R	A	C	E
C	E	N	T	■	W	A	R	P	S	■	E	U	R	O
S	E	A	T	M	A	T	E	S	■	P	E	C	A	N
■	■	N	E	U	T	E	R	■	D	O	Z	E	N	S
S	M	A	R	T	E	D	■	A	A	R	E	■	■	■
T	I	P	J	A	R	■	B	U	M	S	■	C	R	U
P	A	E	A	N	■	B	O	D	A	C	I	O	U	S
A	T	E	I	T	■	I	R	I	S	H	M	O	S	S
T	A	L	L	S	■	B	E	E	K	E	E	P	E	R

21

F	L	E	W	B	Y	■	G	E	S	T	A	T	E	S
R	E	D	H	O	T	■	A	L	T	E	R	A	N	T
I	N	W	A	R	D	■	Z	I	P	D	R	I	V	E
E	N	O	L	A	■	T	E	X	A	S	■	L	I	T
Z	O	O	E	X	H	I	B	I	T	■	T	O	S	S
E	N	D	S	■	O	D	O	R	■	M	A	R	I	O
■	■	■	P	R	E	S	■	S	E	X	T	O	N	■
H	E	R	A	L	D	S	■	L	E	G	I	O	N	S
O	P	A	Q	U	E	■	L	E	E	S	■	■	■	■
M	I	N	U	S	■	T	E	A	M	■	S	A	S	S
E	S	A	I	■	G	R	A	P	E	J	E	L	L	Y
P	O	L	■	G	R	I	F	T	■	U	P	P	E	D
O	D	O	N	N	E	L	L	■	O	M	A	H	A	N
R	E	N	T	A	B	L	E	■	A	B	L	A	Z	E
T	I	G	H	T	E	S	T	■	F	O	S	S	E	Y

22

C	O	R	N	C	O	B	P	I	P	E	■	T	A	M
O	N	A	C	A	R	O	U	S	E	L	■	A	L	E
R	A	N	A	N	E	R	R	A	N	D	■	K	T	S
G	I	G	A	■	D	R	O	N	E	B	E	E	S	■
I	R	E	■	A	W	E	■	A	R	E	A	R	■	■
■	■	S	T	A	R	D	O	M	■	T	I	N	S	■
S	P	H	I	N	X	L	I	K	E	■	A	M	A	H
Y	O	U	D	O	■	I	C	E	■	O	R	A	T	E
N	O	D	E	■	I	N	T	E	G	R	A	T	E	D
E	L	S	A	■	T	E	A	C	O	Z	Y	■	■	■
■	T	O	R	T	E	■	H	B	O	■	S	U	B	■
S	A	N	M	A	R	I	N	O	■	C	A	S	E	■
E	B	B	■	D	A	N	U	B	E	R	I	V	E	R
A	L	A	■	A	N	C	I	E	N	T	R	O	M	E
U	E	Y	■	S	T	A	T	E	S	E	C	R	E	T

23

W	H	O	A	■	P	R	I	M	A	L	U	R	G	E
H	A	R	M	■	L	E	G	A	L	I	Z	E	I	T
A	B	A	B	■	I	D	O	B	E	L	I	E	V	E
T	A	L	E	S	E	■	T	E	X	T	■	F	E	R
I	N	E	R	T	■	A	Y	L	A	■	R	E	I	N
S	E	X	S	Y	M	B	O	L	■	L	O	R	N	E
I	R	A	■	L	U	L	U	■	C	U	T	■	■	■
T	O	M	K	I	T	E	■	D	U	C	H	A	M	P
■	■	I	S	T	■	P	O	R	K	■	N	A	E	■
D	E	A	T	H	■	P	A	T	T	Y	C	A	K	E
O	N	E	S	■	K	E	N	S	■	M	O	T	E	L
O	R	R	■	T	H	E	O	■	K	E	N	O	B	I
F	I	O	N	A	A	P	P	L	E	■	E	L	A	N
U	C	B	E	R	K	E	L	E	Y	■	Y	I	N	G
S	H	E	S	A	I	D	Y	E	S	■	S	A	K	S

24

C	O	L	B	E	R	T	B	U	M	P	■	C	H	E
E	V	E	R	S	O	S	O	R	R	Y	■	O	A	R
L	E	G	I	S	L	A	T	U	R	E	■	N	I	N
T	R	O	T	■	A	R	S	■	O	D	I	S	T	S
■	■	■	I	N	S	■	M	A	O	S	U	I	T	■
A	S	G	A	R	D	■	V	I	R	G	I	L	■	■
H	E	E	L	S	■	D	A	R	K	S	T	A	R	S
A	L	O	E	■	H	A	S	T	E	■	A	T	O	I
B	A	C	K	B	E	N	C	H	■	F	R	E	O	N
■	■	A	S	I	A	G	O	■	S	E	T	S	T	O
D	O	C	E	N	T	S	■	B	A	Y	■	■	■	■
O	N	H	I	G	H	■	O	A	F	■	A	W	E	S
L	I	I	■	H	E	A	T	S	E	N	S	O	R	S
C	O	N	■	A	R	C	T	I	C	O	C	E	A	N
E	N	G	■	M	Y	C	O	L	O	G	I	S	T	S

25

L	E	S	S	C	O	M	P	L	I	C	A	T	E	D
O	N	E	A	F	T	E	R	A	N	O	T	H	E	R
T	H	E	G	O	B	L	E	T	O	F	F	I	R	E
H	A	T	E	S	■	D	W	A	R	F	■	E	I	S
A	N	O	S	■	D	I	R	K	■	E	L	V	E	S
I	C	I	■	K	E	N	A	I	■	R	E	E	S	E
R	E	T	■	E	G	G	P	A	N	■	E	S	T	D
■	■	I	G	A	■	■	U	A	R	■	■	■	■	■
S	N	C	C	■	S	O	M	B	E	R	■	I	C	E
C	O	L	O	R	■	S	I	E	V	E	■	N	A	Y
A	T	O	N	E	■	M	A	J	A	■	H	A	M	E
C	A	S	■	S	P	O	S	E	■	B	A	S	E	L
C	L	E	A	N	A	S	A	W	H	I	S	T	L	E
H	O	S	T	I	L	E	R	E	A	C	T	I	O	N
I	T	T	A	K	E	S	A	L	L	S	O	R	T	S

26

C	A	M	P	■	H	O	W	D	A	R	E	Y	O	U
E	V	E	R	■	I	N	A	U	G	U	R	A	L	S
D	I	D	O	■	M	E	L	O	N	B	A	L	L	S
A	L	I	T	O	■	A	T	S	E	A	■	E	A	R
R	A	C	E	C	A	R	D	■	W	T	S	■	■	■
■	■	■	S	U	M	M	I	T	■	O	K	B	U	T
E	A	S	T	L	A	■	S	E	W	■	Y	O	K	E
C	A	L	V	I	N	A	N	D	H	O	B	B	E	S
O	R	E	O	■	A	C	E	■	A	T	O	A	S	T
N	E	W	T	O	■	H	Y	D	R	O	X	■	■	■
■	■	■	E	R	N	■	W	I	F	E	S	W	A	P
A	R	T	■	L	I	M	O	S	■	S	E	E	M	E
R	E	T	R	O	V	I	R	U	S	■	A	W	A	R
A	N	Y	O	N	E	E	L	S	E	■	T	O	T	O
B	E	L	T	S	A	N	D	E	R	■	S	N	I	T

27

A	D	J	A	C	E	N	T	T	O	■	S	M	U	G
D	R	O	P	A	N	C	H	O	R	■	P	E	T	E
V	O	C	A	L	C	O	R	D	S	■	A	N	T	A
I	L	K	S	■	S	S	E	■	■	U	N	S	E	R
L	L	O	S	A	■	■	E	M	I	R	■	C	R	T
■	■	■	■	M	I	S	D	O	N	E	■	H	M	O
C	R	E	D	I	T	C	A	R	D	■	O	O	O	O
D	E	N	T	A	L	H	Y	G	I	E	N	I	S	T
P	D	A	S	■	L	O	W	E	R	B	E	R	T	H
L	A	M	■	A	D	R	E	N	A	L	■	■	■	■
A	L	E	■	W	O	R	E	■	■	A	L	L	A	H
Y	E	L	L	S	■	■	K	T	S	■	E	E	R	O
E	R	L	E	■	P	E	E	R	R	E	V	I	E	W
R	T	E	S	■	U	S	N	A	T	I	O	N	A	L
S	S	R	S	■	B	A	D	M	A	N	N	E	R	S

28

C	R	E	E	P	S	H	O	W	■	S	C	I	F	I
H	E	D	G	E	M	A	Z	E	■	A	U	D	E	N
A	L	M	O	D	O	V	A	R	■	P	R	E	S	S
N	Y	U	■	S	K	E	W	E	D	■	T	O	T	O
G	O	N	G	■	I	N	A	W	A	Y	■	L	I	L
E	N	D	R	U	N	■	■	O	N	E	L	O	V	E
■	■	■	A	N	G	■	F	L	A	R	E	G	U	N
C	A	S	T	E	■	E	L	F	■	T	R	Y	S	T
A	C	T	I	V	E	L	Y	■	P	L	O	■	■	■
P	H	O	N	E	M	E	■	R	E	U	B	E	N	■
Y	I	N	■	N	A	V	A	J	O	■	X	O	X	O
B	E	E	S	■	G	E	L	A	T	O	■	N	O	D
A	V	A	N	T	■	N	E	F	E	R	T	I	T	I
R	E	G	A	N	■	T	R	A	U	M	A	T	I	C
A	D	E	P	T	■	H	O	R	S	E	R	A	C	E

29

C	A	B	O	T	■	R	P	M	S	■	D	A	W	G
A	L	A	N	A	■	E	R	A	T	■	O	P	A	L
L	A	D	Y	G	O	D	I	V	A	■	R	I	L	E
I	M	A	X	■	N	A	M	E	B	R	A	N	D	S
F	O	P	■	A	C	E	R	■	E	G	G	O	S	■
■	■	P	I	N	S	T	R	I	P	E	S	■	■	■
H	O	L	D	U	P	■	S	C	A	B	■	B	E	A
M	A	E	S	T	R	O	■	K	R	O	G	E	R	S
O	K	S	■	T	E	N	S	■	A	K	I	T	A	S
■	■	■	F	R	E	E	P	A	S	S	E	S	■	■
O	S	S	I	E	■	S	I	M	I	■	■	Y	M	A
W	H	O	L	E	W	H	E	A	T	■	E	R	O	S
L	O	U	T	■	H	A	L	T	E	R	T	O	P	S
E	R	S	E	■	O	R	E	O	■	A	T	S	E	A
T	E	A	R	■	M	E	R	L	■	M	E	S	S	Y

30

B	U	Z	Z	K	I	L	L	■	M	E	T	A	L
O	N	I	O	N	S	O	U	P	■	A	G	A	P	E
T	E	N	N	I	S	A	C	E	■	L	A	Y	N	E
■	■	■	E	T	O	N	■	S	T	I	L	L	E	R
G	A	T	S	■	■	E	C	O	N	■	O	A	S
U	G	H	■	G	O	S	S	I	P	G	I	R	L
A	R	E	Y	O	U	O	K	■	S	E	P	S	■
C	A	H	O	O	T	S	■	S	P	R	A	W	L	S
■	■	A	R	G	O	■	P	R	I	E	D	I	E	U
■	O	N	E	O	F	A	K	I	N	D	■	F	I	N
I	N	G	■	O	I	L	S	■	■	S	T	A	G
C	L	O	S	E	T	S	■	O	M	N	I	■
O	Y	V	E	Y	■	A	R	R	A	I	G	N	E	D
S	I	E	G	E	■	B	E	E	N	T	H	E	R	E
A	F	R	O	S	■	D	O	N	E	T	H	A	T

31

```
S M O O T H J A Z Z ■ G M A C
H E R E S T O Y O U ■ R A B E
I N T R A M U R A L ■ A T I T
V U E ■ R L S ■ U R B A N A
E D G E S ■ T E S S A ■ H I C
R O A D ■ O S L O ■ S P A T E
■ ■ K A N ■ E U P H O R I A
A L L O V E R C R E A T I O N
P E A C E O U T ■ P D A ■ ■
O N T H E ■ N E T S ■ T A N A
S A E ■ N O T D O ■ N O B E L
T O R P O R ■ ■ W E E ■ R E B
A L M A ■ A C C E S S C O D E
T I A S ■ N E A R A T H A N D
E N N A ■ G E T S U S E D T O
```

32

```
G A B Y ■ S T O O D I N F O R
O M O O ■ K E P T A D I A R Y
T O N G ■ O R E O C O O K I E
C R E A M R I N S E ■ B E E S
H E R M I T ■ ■ ■ P E N N E
A S S A D ■ P A R D O ■ A T E
■ ■ T W E E Z E R S ■ M A D
O R B ■ I N S T A N T ■ E L S
M I L ■ V I C E C O P S ■ ■
E C U ■ E D I C T ■ A P E R S
L E E D S ■ ■ B I L L E T
E C H O ■ P H O T O D I O D E
T H E O R I O L E S ■ T I L E
T E N N E S S E A N ■ U S E D
E X S E N A T O R S ■ P E G S
```

33

```
U P I N A R M S ■ M A S S E S
D O M I N I C A ■ O C T O P I
D R A G O N E T ■ O N E N I L
E T C H ■ D W Y A N E W A D E
R I O ■ T S A R S ■ S T U N
■ A P I A ■ N I T T I ■ I R T
■ ■ C N N ■ C R I M I N A L
S T P E T E R ■ A N O M A L Y
C H A T R O O M ■ E N A ■ ■
H E Y ■ A N N A S ■ I C B M
E L I S ■ I N P U T ■ E E L
D O N T J I N X I T ■ F E T A
U R G E O N ■ C R U D I T E S
L A U R E N ■ A E R O F L O T
E X P E L S ■ T A N G I E R S
```

34

```
F E S T I V U S ■ A F F I R M
O V E R R I D E ■ V I E F O R
G E T A R O O M ■ E R A S E S
G R A V E L ■ I N N E R ■ ■
■ ■ E G A D ■ O U T ■ P D A
D M V ■ S I S T E R H O O D
R E E F S ■ S A S Q U A T C H
E N L A I ■ E C O ■ C R A K E
S A C K L U N C H ■ K I T E R
S C R E E N D O O R ■ O D E
Y E O ■ N G O ■ T W I T ■ ■
■ ■ S T O W S ■ A R O M A S
B A S T E D ■ P U N K R O C K
I T G I R L ■ U N D E R W A Y
T V T R A Y ■ D E A D E N D S
```

35

```
S T A R ■ T R A C T ■ C P A S
T O N E ■ H A G E R ■ H I V E
O R A N G E S O D A ■ I N E Z
P O T E N T ■ G E N T L E R ■
S N O W C A P ■ Q U I T I T
A T M S ■ K E P T ■ R O A L D
T O Y ■ G I R L I E G I R L S
■ ■ J U N K E M A I L ■ ■
S T R A N G E B I R D ■ G I B
O W E N S ■ D E N T ■ S O S A
T O S S I N ■ G H E T T O S
■ P O T T A G E ■ S E R A P E
M A L E ■ R E Q U I R E S O F
R I V E ■ Y O U N G ■ W A D E
T R E N ■ A S I A N ■ N Y S E
```

36

```
I C A N N O T T E L L A L I E
M O N E Y F O R N O T H I N G
P R I V A T E E N T R A N C E
A R M E D ░ S M U T S ░ E L S
L E A R ░ W H O I S ░ S O O T
A C T ░ D I O R S ░ S C U S E
S T E A R N E S ░ S E A T E D
░ ░ ░ R I D S ░ P O E M ░ ░ ░
T B O N E S ░ H A N D S A W S
A R I E S ░ C A R D S ░ L A H
P E L L ░ C O M T E ░ A B R I
I N B ░ R A L L Y ░ E N U R E
O N E C E L L E D A N I M A L
C A L C U L A T I N G M I N D
A N T I P E R S P I R A N T S
```

37

```
B U B B L E U P ░ O F F S E T
O P E R E T T A ░ D R O P I T
S T A R S H I P ░ D I N E R O
H O U R ░ A C E S ░ A D R E P
░ ░ ░ ░ S N A R E D R U M ░ ░
C A P O T E ░ B A A ░ E D I T
F L E E R ░ S A N T A ░ O R R
L E N N O N M C C A R T N E Y
A R A ░ H O O K E ░ P E O N S
T O L D ░ D O W ░ S E C R E T
░ ░ T H E S T R O L L ░ ░ ░ ░
B R Y A N ░ H I F I ░ D I T Z
R U B R I C ░ T A N Z A N I A
A L O M A R ░ E G G I N G O N
T E X A C O ░ R E S T E A S Y
```

38

```
D U M M Y B A G ░ ░ S C A M S
A N Y D A Y N O W ░ T O N I C
W H O S H O T J R ░ L Y N C H
N I P ░ ░ B R U I S E ░ A R M
S P E R M ░ A M T O O ░ M O A
░ ░ O A F ░ P E W ░ B A W L ░
░ Q U O V A D I S ░ M A R A T
P U T T I N O N T H E R I T Z
L I T E S ░ S T O O D P A T ░
A V E R ░ A S H ░ P E I ░ ░ ░
Y E R ░ I C I E R ░ A N N E S
A R F ░ T H E L O T ░ U N H ░
R I O T S ░ R A D I O C O D E
E N O R M ░ S K I N D I V E R
A G L E Y ░ ░ E N S E N A D A
```

39

```
F R E N E M I E S ░ D E C A L
R E V E R E N C E ░ E X I L E
I C E C A S T L E ░ D F L A T
T A N K S ░ L A N C E B A S S
O N E S E C ░ I T O ░ I N T R
S T D ░ ░ H U R O N S ░ T A O
░ ░ ░ C H U G S ░ C E D R I C
D J B O O T H ░ N E W Y O R K
J U A R E Z ░ H O R S E ░ ░ ░
O N T ░ S P R I N T ░ ░ R A M
K I T T ░ A O L ░ S A L U T E
O P E R A H A T S ░ C O L O N
V E N A L ░ D O Y O U M I N D
I R E N E ░ I N S U R A N C E
C O D E X ░ E S T R A N G E D
```

40

```
A I R Q U O T E S ░ ░ M P A A
C H E A T S H E E T ░ Y O S T
H O T T A M A L E S ░ A S T I
E P A ░ H A L ░ P U R I T A N
S E I S ░ N I P ░ N A M I N G
O N N O W ░ A Q U A V I T A E
N O E V I L ░ R A M I S ░ ░ ░
░ T R I N E S ░ W I N T E R ░
░ ░ ░ E G E S T ░ S E R I E S
W A T T M E T E R ░ D U G A T
A M O R A L ░ D E L ░ E H L E
R O T U N D A ░ F O X ░ T S E
A R A B ░ E X X O N M O B I L
C E L L ░ R E O R G A N I Z E
E S S E ░ ░ D O M I N A T E S
```

41

```
I N S T A G R A M ■ Q A T A R
H A T E C R I M E ■ V E R G E
A M I N O A C I D ■ C I E R A
D E C ■ W I T S ■ ■ O N E D
A N K H ■ N U T S ■ C U T E Y
B A T O N ■ S A L A R Y ■ ■
A M O S O Z ■ D O M E ■ G N C
L E I P Z I G ■ T O P S O I L
L S T ■ Z O R A ■ R E T I N A
■ ■ E L N I N O ■ S A T A Y
S K Y P E ■ T A L C ■ T A R A
T R O I ■ ■ T E E M ■ L I I
R E U P S ■ L O O S E R O C K
A M I E L ■ A L L A T O N C E
P E N N Y ■ B E E R S T E I N
```

42

```
L O N G A R M ■ M A S H E D
A P O L L O I ■ I L L M A D E
S T T I T U S ■ R I L E D U P
S E N N E T T ■ R I O T A C T
E D I T ■ S E G A ■ F A T A H
R I C E ■ R I T E ■ N I T S
■ N E D S ■ M A I N G A T E ■
■ ■ T A X C O D E ■ ■
■ G O E A S Y O N ■ O B I E
B A U M ■ O Z M A ■ I S N T
A Z T E C ■ P O L S ■ R I M A
R E F R A C T ■ F A K E T A N
C L A I R O L ■ E Y E M A S K
A L L T A L K ■ A S P E R S E
R E L A T E ■ R O I S T E R
```

43

```
A F G H A N ■ S K I J U M P ■
M A L A W I ■ M E N E L A U S
B R A Z E N ■ I N S E C U R E
L I N E ■ E N T O ■ R E N E W
E N D ■ P O O H ■ R A G A
D A S H I N G ■ A T F ■ L O G
■ A C E I N T H E H O L E
■ D A W N O F T H E D E A D ■
J A C K I N T H E B O X ■
O R T ■ C E S ■ A R R A I G N
S K I M ■ F R I A ■ M O E
E R V I N ■ M A T T ■ S C A M
P O I S O N E D ■ I M P A L E
H O T H O U S E ■ S C A L I A
■ M Y A N M A R ■ H I T M E N
```

44

```
P I P E D R E A M ■ A R B O L
A N A S T A S I A ■ P I A N O
C U R S E W O R D ■ P O N E S
T I T A N ■ E L U L ■ G S T
S T A Y ■ W A D I S ■ P A P A
■ ■ Y I N ■ B E F A L L S
A M A R E T T I ■ R E C O A T
S O M E T H I N G F I E R C E
I N A P I E ■ G O E S D E E P
F O R E S A W ■ N E T ■ ■
T T Y L ■ S I Z E S ■ P A S T
O R L ■ M E D E ■ D E W A R
S E L M A ■ O B A M A C A R E
A M I T Y ■ W R I T L A R G E
Y E S N O ■ S A M M E N D E S
```

45

```
G S H A R P ■ C A S T I R O N
E C O C A R ■ A L P A C I N O
O R T E G A ■ T I E L I N E S
R A H ■ E N H A N C E ■ G P A
G M E N ■ K A L E S ■ N E I L
O J A Y S ■ N O S ■ V E R N E
H E D G E H O G ■ F E W ■ ■
M T S I N A I ■ F A L S E S T
■ ■ A D J ■ S E Q U E N C E
I C O N S ■ V E L ■ M U T E R
M O L T ■ K E V I N ■ M I N A
B C D ■ A N N E X E S ■ C A W
I C E Q U E E N ■ E L M I R A
B Y S T R E E T ■ D A R N I T
E X T R A D R Y ■ S P I G O T
```

46

```
H A L F A N D H A L F ■ C C S
I N A U G U R A T O R ■ A L I
N I N J A T U R T L E ■ P A N
D O D I ■ M E N L O P A R K
I N S ■ W C S ■ ■ O N I C E ■
■ C E E ■ A L P ■ A I M S
■ S H O E L A C E ■ Z Z T O P
C H A N D L E R A R I Z O N A
H I S S Y ■ R I P A P A R T ■
I N D O ■ H O D ■ U P S ■
■ T I L D E ■ F L Y ■ C C L
T O B E E X A C T ■ E L I E
H I S ■ C A V E D R A W I N G
O S O ■ A N I D I F R A N C O
R M N ■ F E D E X K I N K O S
```

47

```
S T E E R I N G C L E A R O F
C A R B O N F O O T P R I N T
I S T A N D C O R R E C T E D
■ K E Y S ■ T D S ■ E S T D ■
■ ■ E L A ■
A S T H E S A Y I N G G O E S
B A R E X A M ■ R I H A N N A
I C E R U N ■ T O R E A T
D R E A D E D ■ R E U N I T E
E A S T E R N A I R L I N E S
■ A D P ■
F A C E ■ T O O ■ M S R P
D I S A S T E R S U P P O R T
E X E R C I S E T R A I N E R
N E A R E S T R E L A T I V E
```

48

```
T R I T T ■ S C R A M ■ A B A
V I R E O ■ C H I N A ■ N O R
P T O L E M A I C S Y S T E M
G E N E R A L ■ ■ B E E R S
■ R E P U L S E R
G O S ■ N E E ■ V W S
V A N E S S A W I L L I A M S
E L E C T E D O F F I C I A L
N A R R A T I V E P O E T R Y
A T E E N A G E R I N L O V E
L I E C H T E N S T E I N E R
■ A D I O ■ I S S E L ■
E P E E ■ R E S T S O N
H O R S E M A N U R E ■ E U R
A L E ■ S U C C E S S ■ C S A
Y D S ■ S H O D
```

49

```
M A K E P E A C E ■ A D E N I
A L E X A N D R A ■ T R Y O N
H A P P Y D A Y S ■ E J E C T
A N T I S ■ P E R I ■ S H E
L I A R ■ P A T B E N A T A R
O S T E ■ L L O Y D ■ L A N I
■ L O D Z ■ D E L C O
W O O D Y W O O D P E C K E R
I S S U E ■ O R A L ■
N O M E ■ A F L A T ■ A P B S
C L O S E Q U O T E ■ N E E T
H E S ■ W I N G ■ A D L A I
E M I L E ■ G I R L G R O U P
L I N E R ■ U S H E R E T T E
L O G O S ■ S T O W A W A Y S
```

50

```
S I G H T I N G ■ J A R F U L
A S L O O S E A S A G O O S E
C H A I N L I N K F E N C E S
H A M S ■ E N D E A R ■ A R S
E L I T E ■ E E R ■ A C N E
M L S ■ C O U R T ■ P E C A N
■ F O R M S ■ D O T I M E
I A C O C C A ■ H E N N A E D
C L A R A S ■ H O N D A ■
A L T A R ■ L A T T E ■ C S A
N O S Y ■ C U B ■ R E A C T
T C U ■ P A N I C S ■ T B A R
W A I T I N G T O E X H A L E
I T T A K E S A L L K I N D S
N E S T E D ■ T E L E C A S T
```

51

J	E	S	U	S	F	I	S	H	■	A	S	S	E	S
O	P	E	R	A	A	R	I	A	■	X	T	I	L	E
B	I	L	L	A	B	O	N	G	■	L	O	C	A	L
S	S	E	■	B	I	N	G	■	■	L	I	N	T	■
A	T	N	O	■	O	I	L	S	■	W	A	L	T	Z
C	L	I	C	K	■	C	E	A	S	E	F	I	R	E
T	E	C	H	I	E	■	T	I	L	T	■	A	A	R
■	■	O	N	E	G	■	L	A	N	A	■	■	■	■
S	T	E	■	G	L	O	B	■	B	A	Z	A	A	R
W	H	A	M	M	Y	B	A	R	■	P	U	L	S	E
E	E	R	I	E	■	I	D	E	D	■	R	I	F	E
E	R	A	S	■	■	D	A	I	S	■	B	A	N	■
P	I	C	T	S	■	T	A	T	T	O	O	A	R	T
E	T	H	E	R	■	S	T	A	T	U	S	B	A	R
A	Z	E	R	A	■	E	A	S	Y	P	E	A	S	Y

52

G	A	Y	P	A	R	A	D	E	■	P	A	R	O	L
O	S	U	L	L	I	V	A	N	■	I	R	I	N	A
R	A	M	A	D	A	I	N	N	■	O	T	O	E	S
D	I	A	N	E	L	A	N	E	■	N	I	G	H	T
O	L	S	O	N	■	T	O	A	■	S	C	R	I	P
■	■	■	■	Z	E	N	D	A	■	L	A	T	E	■
S	W	E	A	T	E	D	■	S	I	L	E	N	T	N
C	E	N	T	E	R	■	■	M	A	I	D	E	N	■
R	I	G	H	T	O	H	■	Q	U	I	V	E	R	Y
E	M	I	L	■	G	A	S	U	P	■	■	■	■	■
W	A	N	E	S	■	R	E	O	■	S	A	D	A	S
B	R	E	T	T	■	D	A	N	C	E	H	A	L	L
A	E	S	I	R	■	M	R	S	T	E	E	V	E	E
C	R	O	C	I	■	A	L	E	R	T	M	I	N	D
K	A	N	S	A	■	N	E	T	L	O	S	S	E	S

53

P	L	A	Y	T	E	X	■	D	O	L	■	A	P	S
V	I	C	T	O	R	Y	■	A	R	A	P	A	H	O
T	E	N	D	R	I	L	■	W	I	M	O	W	E	H
S	U	E	■	T	E	E	N	■	F	E	L	L	A	S
■	■	C	O	S	M	O	G	I	R	L	■	■	■	■
A	S	S	A	I	■	R	O	C	■	O	C	T	A	■
S	T	O	P	S	■	S	T	R	E	T	C	H	E	S
H	E	N	I	E	■	C	H	E	■	I	R	I	S	H
B	A	I	T	S	H	O	P	S	■	M	E	N	L	O
Y	M	C	A	■	A	N	O	■	B	E	G	A	T	■
■	■	L	E	V	E	L	H	E	A	D	■	■	■	■
R	E	G	G	A	E	■	E	A	R	L	■	N	T	H
A	V	I	A	T	O	R	■	U	N	A	W	A	R	E
P	A	T	I	E	N	T	■	N	I	N	E	V	E	H
■	C	A	N	N	E	S	■	T	E	D	D	I	E	S

54

B	A	S	T	I	L	L	E	■	T	O	O	B	A	D
C	A	T	S	M	E	O	W	■	U	N	P	I	L	E
S	H	O	E	L	A	C	E	■	R	E	E	K	O	F
■	■	C	L	O	C	K	S	■	B	I	N	E	T	■
R	A	K	I	S	H	■	■	S	O	R	E	■	■	■
O	N	P	O	T	■	M	A	H	J	O	N	G	G	■
A	C	H	T	■	B	A	R	T	E	N	D	E	R	S
C	H	O	■	C	A	R	P	E	T	S	■	E	A	T
H	O	T	P	O	C	K	E	T	S	■	D	Y	N	E
■	R	O	A	D	K	I	L	L	■	M	E	A	D	E
■	■	■	J	E	T	E	■	■	F	E	S	T	E	R
■	D	E	A	N	A	■	P	L	I	N	T	H	■	■
M	A	D	M	A	X	■	A	I	R	D	R	I	E	D
I	M	G	A	M	E	■	C	A	M	E	O	N	T	O
R	E	E	S	E	S	■	K	R	A	Z	Y	K	A	T

55

F	I	R	E	F	O	X	■	M	O	Z	I	L	L	A
O	N	A	R	A	N	T	■	C	R	O	N	I	E	S
E	X	C	I	T	E	R	■	M	E	N	O	T	T	I
■	S	K	E	E	T	E	R	■	S	E	N	T	I	N
■	■	■	D	O	M	E	S	■	S	I	L	T	■	■
A	L	F	A	■	N	E	A	T	H	■	T	E	L	L
G	O	O	S	E	■	G	L	O	O	M	■	B	O	A
H	A	Z	A	R	D	A	N	O	P	I	N	I	O	N
A	D	Z	■	G	O	M	A	D	■	T	E	R	S	E
S	E	I	S	■	S	E	M	I	S	■	O	D	E	S
■	D	E	M	S	■	S	E	N	T	A	■	■	■	■
R	U	B	A	T	O	■	S	L	E	D	D	O	G	■
A	P	E	L	I	K	E	■	I	P	H	O	N	E	S
G	O	A	L	L	I	N	■	N	O	O	N	E	R	S
U	N	R	A	T	E	D	■	E	N	C	A	S	E	S

56

```
  R O A D S T E R S
  S A M U E L A D A M S
  M I N N E S O T A F A T S
L E N D E R   S T R A T I
I T E R S   S A P   S T P A T
T R A Y   S E N E T   E L K S
T O D   S P L I T S C R E E N
E S O   E E L L I K E   S H O
R E C O N N O I T E R   C O T
E X O N   T U N E D   S E L F
R U N E S   T E S   K I N D A
S A N S E I     W I N T E R
  L O T T E R Y W I N N E R
  R O A S T M A S T E R
    P E T E A C H E R
```

57

```
O L D G E E Z E R   K A P P A
R A R I N T O G O   A L O A D
C H I L D H O O D   Z E P P O
A R P   T I P S   S O C C E R
    P O O L   F L O   U R N
A B L E   P A D D Y   B L T
I R O N M I N E R   P E T I T
D O N T M A K E M E L A U G H
A W G E E   T R E A S U R E R
  N I L   P O E M S   T E R O
O S S   C A N   O T I S
M U L D E R   D R A T   D W I
A G A R S   P O I S O N O A K
H A N N A   T R A I L B I K E
A R D O R   S A L A D A T E A
```

58

```
N I C O L A S C A G E   B A H
A D O B E R E A D E R   A L E
W A R R E N Z E V O N   U T A
  R A I S A   S I S S Y B A R
P E L E   Z E A L   A L I T
B Y R N E   M R P E E P E R S
J O E   M A T   M A L A
S U D S E S     V E T O E S
    P R I G   Y E N   N T H
D A I R Y F A R M   A S T R A
A L F A   L O A M   C H U M
S P I T T O O N   O B O E S
H E M   W O O D F U R N A C E
E R A   I N T E R R A C I A L
S T Y   G A S L A N T E R N S
```

59

```
S T E P S I T U P   T O Q U E
W E L L A W A R E   I N U R N
A L M A M A T E R   G E I S T
M O S T E S T   F R E S C A S
I S T O   H E R   T R E K
    J A R U L E   A B M S
D U C T E D   B E S T S U I T
M C R A E   A B E   B O C C I
A L A N P A G E   H A N K E R
J A Z Z   P A R L O R
  Y A K S   Y U M   L A R A
W H I N I E R   M E N A C E D
H A D I N   E X P L E T I V E
A T E A T   C L E A R E D U P
T H A N E   D V D B O X S E T
```

60

```
S E L E N A G O M E Z   A B S
E M I L Y B R O N T E   U R I
M E S A A R I Z O N A   R E S
I R T   L A N E   A L B E R T
P S I   A M C     O L A F I
R O N A   H O T B U T T O N
O N G O A L   D O E S   E X E
    K N O W I T A L L
E M S   Y E W S   M Y O P E S
G O O U T W I T H   O R N E
G O N N A   E D O   E T C
S N O O K I   W R I T   T E T
A P R   E D D I E A R C A R O
C I A   R E A L T R O O P E R
S E N   S E E D O Y S T E R S
```

61

```
S C R I P T S █ T E A M U S A
P I E R R O T █ S A M O V A R
I N S T O R E █ P R O V E R B
E C O █ M I R Y █ T R E A D S
L O W █ K E N O S H A █ █ █
█ █ M I S █ U T I L I Z E D
S T E I N █ S N E E █ N E R O
T H E A G I N G P R O C E S S
L I L T █ H A G S █ H A S T E
O N S A F A R I █ O P S █ █
█ █ E T E R N A L █ D E M
M A K E M E █ L A K E █ E T A
O R I G A M I █ C L A M B A R
P E D A L E D █ R E S O R T S
S A D D E N S █ E Y E W A S H
```

62

```
D E P O S I T O N L Y █ O D D
U T I L I T Y P O L E █ V I R
B A N A N A C R E A M █ E L Y
S S E █ A S H Y █ N E A R E R
█ █ A T C O █ T E N D S T O
I N D I R A █ M A R I E T T A
C A R L A █ H E R O S █ R A S
E P I S █ T O A D S █ H U N T
L O L █ T E S T Y █ M O N T E
A L L S O R T S █ W A G G E D
N E P A L I S █ W E D S █ █
D O R S E Y █ S A I L █ A L E
E N E █ D A I L Y M I R R O R
R I S █ O K S A N A B A I U L
S I S █ S I L V E R S T A T E
```

63

```
P E A R L J A M █ G A S B A G
A S Q U I E T A S A M O U S E
S T A N D U P S T R A I G H T
D E B T S █ A H I █ L E G
E R A █ C R A M P █ R E N O
█ M A R █ U R S A █
A U T O M O B I L E T I R E S
G R O V E S O F A C A D E M E
U N D E R S T A T E M E N T S
A S S O C I A T E D P R E S S
█ F E N N █ E S S █
L A F F █ G Y R O S █ A H A
E L L █ B I B █ A S S E S
A L E U T I A N I S L A N D S
F O U R W A Y S T O P S I G N
S Y R I A N █ E S T H E T E S
```

64

```
G A R A G E B A N D █ C N B C
O N E C A L O R I E █ R I A L
I N T E R D I C T S █ A C R O
N E E D L E N O S E █ D K N Y
█ █ A R G █ L I L I E S
C A J U N S █ F R E N E M Y █
A W A R D █ B R I C K █ I F S
A H M E █ P L A I T █ O N I T
N I B █ L I O N S █ C H A F E
█ L A M A R C K █ R A M J E T
T E J A N O █ V A L █ █
A B U T █ Z A S I N Z E B R A
L A I T █ H E A D T O T A I L
E C C E █ K O R E A N A R M Y
S K E D █ I N D O N E S I A N
```

65

```
S O B E R E D U P █ M O D E L
A L A N A D A L E █ A L E X A
P E N I N S U L A █ J I L T S
S A D D L E B A G █ O V E R T
█ █ A L E █ R A R E G A S
O N S E T S █ C A P I T A L U
P O E M E █ K E V I N █ T A P
E S A U █ G R E E N █ G O R P
N Y S █ E M A L L █ D I R G E
I P O D N A N O █ C E N S E R
N A N E T T E █ M I X █ █
G R A T E █ P O I N T L E S S
A K B A R █ O R D E R A R M S
C E L I E █ O D D M A N O U T
T R E N D █ L O Y A L I S T S
```

66

```
T H I S I S T R U E █ A S S T
R A C O N T E U R S █ T K O S
I N A R T I S T I C █ T A L K
C E N T E R S █ █ R I A T A S
E S T E R █ H O O S I E R █ █
█ █ R I P V A N W I N K L E █
A N I █ M A U V E █ S T E A L
L A M B █ C L A S H █ S Y M S
A T P A R █ C R E E D █ S P A
N U R S E R A T C H E D █ █ █
█ █ R O S S I N I █ S E L M A
C A V I T Y █ █ R A I S E U P
O L I N █ A N N E B R O N T E
E L S E █ D E A D L E T T E R
N Y E T █ H O W D Y D O O D Y
```

67

```
D R A W E R █ B A S I L I C A
R E M O R A █ A R C H I V A L
E L I J A H █ H A R A K I R I
W O R T █ M A I M █ V E E P S
A S S Y R █ S A I L E D █ █
█ █ L O T T █ S A N T A N A
P A R A G U A Y █ M O O C O W
O R E █ U R B A N I I █ I V A
R I E S E N █ W I N D Y D A Y
T A K E S T O █ G A E A █ █
█ █ A T O N C E █ A N D E S
S A S H A █ F O R T █ G R A M
L O C A T I O N █ R A T I T E
E N I W E T O K █ E C Z E M A
D E S K S E T S █ F E E D E R
```

68

```
A V A I L A B L E C R E D I T
P E R C E N T A G E E R R O R
E N T E N T E C O R D I A L E
S T A R S I N O N E S E Y E S
█ █ █ S E T █ N S A █ █ █ █
J A W █ S A K I █ L A C K E Y
A T A D █ N A C L █ M I L N E
M R L U C K Y █ O C A N A D A
B I D E S █ E M I L █ Q U I T
S P O T T V █ O N E D █ S T S
█ █ █ █ A T O █ A E C █ █ █
A M E R I C A N I N P A R I S
R E G U L A R G A S O L I N E
F E E D I N G O N E S F A C E
S T R E E T A D D R E S S E S
```

69

```
P U R P L E H A Z E █ H S I A
U N D E C L A R E D █ A T O P
S T A N D A L O N E █ B A N S
H O S S █ T O D █ H O R S E
█ █ I D E E █ C H A O S █ █
█ D A V I D S T E I N B E R G
L I N E A █ W E L D █ A A R
I N G █ L A C O S T E █ R N A
E E L █ S L I T █ D E C A F
D R O P O U T O F S I G H T █
█ █ S H A M E █ L U N G █ █
S H A R P █ S I R █ R B I S
H E X A █ P O W E R P O I N T
E R O S █ I M A R E A L B O Y
D O N E █ P A T S Y C L I N E
```

70

```
C R E E P S H O W █ O X B O W
H U R R I C A N E █ L A R G E
O P E N L A N E S █ I N A L L
R E C █ A N D I █ E V A D E D
D E T E S T E D █ X E D █ █
█ O P T █ L A S C R U C E S
B U R I E D █ S T E █ O L E
U N S C R E W █ U P R I G H T
R T E █ M A B █ T E T R I S
B O T T L E C A P █ T E A █
█ V I A █ N E A R M I S S
P O L L E N █ D E M O █ L E I
A R E A S █ B I K I N I W A X
L E A N T █ A T A N Y R A T E
M O N D O █ S O T O M A Y O R
```

71

```
I P H O N E A P P █ D C U P S
M R O L Y M P I A █ E R N I E
P E T E A C H E R █ S E G E R
U M S █ H E I R █ █ D A T E
M I T E █ E D S U L L I V A N
P E O N █ █ █ N A S T A S E
E R N E █ S P L I N T S █
D E E R █ T R I T E █ C O B B
█ █ G R O O V E S █ O P A L
O N L Y Y O U █ █ █ R E N E
L O A D E D D I C E █ E N N E
I B A R █ █ O A S T █ T E D
V A L I D █ C U R S E W O R D
E L A N D █ A S I A N P E A R
S L A K E █ B A B Y D A D D Y
```

72

```
S A L A D B A R █ B A O B A B
A D E Q U A T E █ E S S E N E
V U V U Z E L A █ C A S I T A
E L E A █ Z I L C H █ O N I T
S T E P S █ █ T R E E █ E S P
█ █ L O U D O U T S █ R E O
D I S A S T E R S █ T O R R E
E M A N U E L █ H E A D O U T
A N N E E █ I C E S T O R M S
R O T █ M U L E D E E R █ █
M T A █ E L A L █ S E E Y A
A H A B █ T H I C K █ A L E R
D E N A L I █ C O N S T A N T
A R N H E M █ A L I M E N T S
M E A N T O █ S A T U R D A Y
```

73

```
I N S T A M A T I C █ T H A N
D O O R T O D O O R █ R E P O
I M P A T I E N C E █ Y A P S
G E S █ I S L E █ D E F T L Y
█ █ T R E E █ R E W O V E █
A G R E E S █ S E N O R I T A
G O O N S █ S P E C K █ S I P
A T T N █ S T I L E █ T I N T
S H O █ A P R E S █ R E O I L
P A R A L L E L █ T E E N S Y
█ M O C K U P █ M E D S █
E C O C A R █ D O F F █ Z I P
S I T U █ G U I L L O T I N E
S T E S █ E A S T O R A N G E
E Y R E █ S E C O N D G E A R
```

74

```
█ C H A P █ █ █ P R I M █
V O I C E D █ █ S E E G E R
L E T T E R C █ S T E A N N E
O U T S K I P █ H U R L I N G
G R I M I E R █ A D S I T E S
█ S T A N D T O R E A S O N █
█ E D G A R W I N T E R █
█ █ █ P A I N T █ █
█ H E A R I N G D O G S █
█ H A N G I N G A R O U N D █
L A T T I C E █ B I L L E R S
E V E R T O R █ E V I L E Y E
N O S E A T S █ D E T E R G E
O C T E T S █ █ R E T E A M
█ S O S O █ █ █ S S R S █
```

75

```
A S C H █ C U B A █ B O S N S
S H A Q █ O P E N M A R K E T
T O N S █ L E N T I L S O U P
R E V █ S A N J O S E █ A R A
O S A M A █ D I N G █ C L O T
█ S A Y I █ █ O M A █ █
N A T I O N A L A V E R A G E
I W A N N A B E S E D A T E D
P E R M A N E N T R E C O R D
S E P A R A T E I N C O M E S
█ █ S A S █ █ S A L E █ █
J O L T █ Y E G G █ D E G A S
E X E █ E L N O R T E █ O B E
T I N A T U R N E R █ R Y A N
E D D I E M O N E Y █ F A T S
R E S T S █ N A D A █ K N E E
```

The New York Times

Crossword Puzzles

The #1 Name in Crosswords

Available at your local bookstore or online at nytimes.com/nytstore

St. Martin's Griffin